Poverty in John Steinbeck's *The Pearl*

Other Books in the Social Issues in Literature Series:

Social Issues in Literature

Poverty in John Steinbeck's *The Pearl*

Louise Hawker, Book Editor

GREENHAVEN PRESS
A part of Gale, Cengage Learning

GALE
CENGAGE Learning·

Detroit • New York • San Francisco • New Haven, Conn • Waterville, Maine • London

GALE
CENGAGE Learning·

Elizabeth Des Chenes, *Managing Editor*

© 2012 Greenhaven Press, a part of Gale, Cengage Learning

Gale and Greenhaven Press are registered trademarks used herein under license.

For more information, contact:
Greenhaven Press
27500 Drake Rd.
Farmington Hills, MI 48331-3535
Or you can visit our Internet site at gale.cengage.com

For product information and technology assistance, contact us at

Gale Customer Support, 1-800-877-4253
For permission to use material from this text or product, submit all requests online at www.cengage.com/permissions

Further permissions questions can be emailed to permissionrequest@cengage.com

Articles in Greenhaven Press anthologies are often edited for length to meet page requirements. In addition, original titles of these works are changed to clearly present the main thesis and to explicitly indicate the author's opinion. Every effort is made to ensure that Greenhaven Press accurately reflects the original intent of the authors. Every effort has been made to trace the owners of copyrighted material.

Cover image copyright © Everett Collection/Alamy.

LIBRARY OF CONGRESS CATALOGING-IN-PUBLICATION DATA

Poverty in John Steinbeck's The pearl. / Louise Hawker, book editor.
p. cm. -- (Social issues in literature)
Includes bibliographical references and index.
ISBN 978-0-7377-5807-8 (hardcover) -- ISBN 978-0-7377-5808-5 (pbk.)
1. Steinbeck, John, 1902-1968. Pearl. 2. Poverty in literature. I. Hawker, Louise.
PS3537.T3234P495 2012
813'.52--dc23
2011036481

Printed in Mexico
1 2 3 4 5 6 7 15 14 13 12

Contents

Chapter 1: Background on John Steinbeck

Chapter 2: *The Pearl* and Poverty

Chapter 3: Contemporary Perspectives on Poverty

A US Border Patrol officer's fatal shooting of a fifteen-year-old Mexican boy who was playing with friends focused attention on the violent nature of life in the area and the abuses of poor immigrants by US authorities.

Introduction

In one slim novel, *The Pearl*, John Steinbeck managed to address poverty, wealth, greed, prejudice, racism, and gender equality. At the same time, his prose paints a vivid portrait of the life and environment of a Mexican village. This parable about poor people in a humble setting evokes comparison to current issues. In fact, given the social, political, and economic tumult of recent years, *The Pearl* and its themes still resonate in the twenty-first century.

In spite of these attributes, *The Pearl* did not meet with general acclaim when it was first published in 1945 as "The Pearl of the World" in *Woman's Home Companion*. Some critics belittled it for the fact that it originally appeared in a women's magazine rather than as a book. The story came out in book form as *The Pearl* in 1947, timed for release with a motion picture adaptation. Warren French, a critic and Steinbeck scholar, criticized the book as "lacking insight and worth" and accused Steinbeck of writing the story just to earn money.

Other and more recent literary reviews have been much kinder to *The Pearl*. While critics such as John Timmerman have said that Steinbeck's post–World War II writing is largely dull, *The Pearl* has been praised as a return to Steinbeck's best writing—simple and concise, yet rich with layers of symbolism. That resurgence of quality in Steinbeck's work may have been influenced by his need to express his dismay over the changes in the United States after the war.

As Richard Astro states in the *Gale Dictionary of Literary Biography*, "Steinbeck's organismal view of life, his belief that men can work together to fashion a better, more productive, and more meaningful life, seemed less and less applicable to the world he saw around him." Steinbeck's concern with America's increasingly materialistic values provided impetus for the themes of *The Pearl*. In his essay "From the Tidepool to the Stars: Steinbeck's Sense of Place," Astro writes,

> Steinbeck challenged the celebration of quantity which inheres in every aspect of American life from the structure of our economic and political institutions down to the social lives of individuals. He became skeptical of human ambition and the competition for advantage. . . . He condemned the man-centered attitude toward the environment fostered by the Judeo-Christian ethic. . . . He replaced it with some very simple notions about man's relationship with his place, which are recognized by preliterate peoples (such as the Indians of the Sea of Cortez).

Thus, in the parable of a peasant's encounter with potential wealth, Steinbeck could explore the impact of materialism on a previously simple life. Steinbeck himself said, "When our species progresses toward extinction or marches into the forehead of God, there will be certain degenerate groups left behind, say the Indians of Lower California, who may remain to sun themselves, to eat and starve and sleep and reproduce." Some may take this statement as proof of Steinbeck's stereotyping of Mexicans. But it can also be interpreted as an expression of his view that humans need to live simply instead of pursuing the accumulation of wealth.

The Mexico that Steinbeck knew and depicted in the 1940s was quite different from the Mexico we know in the twenty-first century. The life of Kino and Juana, as portrayed by Steinbeck, was still common in the small villages of Mexico. According to Stephen R. Niblo, author of *Mexico in the 1940s: Modernity, Politics and Corruption*, in 1940 there was only one Mexican for every five who live in that nation now. It was a sparsely populated country, with fewer than ten people per square kilometer. "For the rural majority," writes Niblo," there was a considerable degree of isolation. . . . The village remained the center of the world." Niblo also notes that electrification had not yet come to most rural areas: "In small villages and in the countryside, the dark of night enveloped everything." So the shadows and darkness in *The Pearl*, and the relationship to nature's cycles, are both symbolic and actual. Villagers traveled by foot or used horses or burros— much as Kino and Juana do—and their world, by necessity, was small.

It is fair to say that other than in some Southwest urban areas, the average American likely knew little of Mexico, Mexicans, or even Mexican Americans in the 1940s. Mexico itself experienced a so-called economic miracle as a result of its collaboration with the United States during World War II. In addition, Mexican Americans had the highest percentage of Congressional Medal of Honor winners of any US minority. Mexicans who remained in the United States after the war found an improved quality of life, including access to education via the G.I. Bill, and opportunities to purchase homes. They were spurred to pursue the American dream as well as work to end discrimination.

According to 2010 US Census Bureau data, Hispanics now account for 50 million people in the United States, making them the largest minority group in the nation. One can only speculate about how Steinbeck would view the current status of Mexican Americans and the risks many of them take to forge a new and better life in the United States.

Chronology

1902

John Ernst Steinbeck III is born on February 27 in Salinas, California, to John Ernst and Olive Steinbeck, the only son and third of four children.

1918

Steinbeck becomes gravely ill with pneumonia as a result of the flu epidemic that swept the nation. His lungs would remain vulnerable for the rest of his life.

1919

Steinbeck graduates from Salinas High School in June and enrolls in Stanford University starting in the fall term. He attends sporadically for the next six years.

1920

Steinbeck's father arranges for his summer job with Spreckels, a sugar company, as a maintenance man. Steinbeck meets the Mexican workers who will later serve as inspiration for the characters in his novel *Tortilla Flat*.

1925

Steinbeck leaves Stanford University and heads for New York City, working as a hand on a ship headed through the Panama Canal. In New York he initially finds a job as a construction laborer and eventually as a reporter for the *New York American* newspaper.

1926

Fired from his newspaper job, Steinbeck returns to California and moves to Lake Tahoe to work as caretaker for a summer home. The Lake Tahoe area becomes his home for several years.

1929

Steinbeck publishes his first novel, *Cup of Gold*, and meets Carol Henning, who provides his introduction to the Socialist movement and left-wing politics of the day.

1930

Steinbeck marries Carol Henning, whose politics and social conscience heavily influence Steinbeck and his work throughout the 1930s. The Steinbecks, nearly broke, move to Pacific Grove, California. There Steinbeck meets marine biologist Edward F. Ricketts, who becomes his closest friend for two decades.

1932

Steinbeck publishes *Pastures of Heaven*. The devastating Dust Bowl drought begins in the American Midwest.

1933

Steinbeck publishes *To a God Unknown*.

1934

Steinbeck's mother, Olive, dies in February.

1935

Steinbeck experiences the turning point in his career with the publication of *Tortilla Flat*, which becomes a major success.

1936

Steinbeck publishes *In Dubious Battle* and writes a series of articles on migrant workers for the *San Francisco News*. Steinbeck's father dies.

1937

Steinbeck publishes *Of Mice and Men* and *The Red Pony*. He makes his first trip to Europe and Russia. *Of Mice and Men* opens as a play.

1938

Steinbeck writes *The Grapes of Wrath* in one hundred days between June and October, succumbing to exhaustion at the end of that period. He buys his ranch in Los Gatos, California; he also receives the New York Drama Critics' Circle Award for the theatrical version of *Of Mice and Men*.

1939

The Grapes of Wrath is published and inspires both positive and negative criticism.

1940

The Grapes of Wrath earns Steinbeck the Pulitzer Prize. Film versions of this novel and *Of Mice and Men* are released. Steinbeck and his marine biologist friend Ed Ricketts make a research trip to the Sea of Cortez (Gulf of California) in Mexico.

1941

Steinbeck and Ricketts publish *Sea of Cortez*, a study of the fauna in the Gulf of California.

1942

Steinbeck publishes *The Moon Is Down*. The film version of *Tortilla Flat* is released.

1943

Steinbeck and Carol Henning divorce. Steinbeck marries Gwendolyn Conger.

1944

Steinbeck's first son, Thomas (Thom), is born.

1945

Steinbeck and Gwendolyn move to New York City. *Cannery Row* is published. The film version of *The Moon Is Down* is released. Steinbeck travels to Europe and North Africa as a war correspondent for the *New York Herald Tribune*.

1946

Steinbeck's son John IV is born.

1947

The Wayward Bus and *The Pearl* are published. Steinbeck tours Russia with photographer Robert Capa.

1948

The film version of *The Pearl* is released. Steinbeck publishes *A Russian Journal*. He is elected to the American Academy of Letters. In a tumultuous year, Ed Ricketts dies, and Steinbeck and Gwendolyn divorce.

1950

Steinbeck publishes *Burning Bright,* which also opens as a play, and writes the script for *Viva Zapata!* He marries his third wife, Elaine Scott.

1951

Steinbeck publishes *Log from the Sea of Cortez.*

1952

East of Eden is published; the film version of *Viva Zapata!* is released.

1954

Steinbeck publishes *Sweet Thursday,* a sequel to *Cannery Row.*

1955

The film version of *East of Eden,* starring James Dean, is released.

1957

The Short Reign of Pippin IV is published and the film version of *The Wayward Bus* is released.

1958

Steinbeck publishes *Once There Was a War*.

1960

Steinbeck visits forty states as he travels across America with his poodle Charley.

1961

Steinbeck publishes *The Winter of Our Discontent*.

1962

Steinbeck receives the Nobel Prize for Literature; *Travels with Charley* is published.

1963

Steinbeck travels to Scandinavia, Eastern Europe, and Russia, where he is very popular and his work is well known.

1964

Steinbeck is awarded the United States Medal of Freedom.

1965

Steinbeck covers the Vietnam War for Long Island *Newsday*. His son John is drafted into the US Army and serves in Vietnam.

1966

America and the Americans, a series of travel essays with blunt commentary by Steinbeck, who is quite ill, is published.

1968

Steinbeck dies on December 20 and is buried in Salinas, California.

Background on John Steinbeck

The Life of John Steinbeck

Richard Astro

Richard Astro is provost emeritus and Distinguished Professor of English at Drexel University in Philadelphia. He has authored several books on John Steinbeck. His disciplines include twentieth-century American fiction, eighteenth-century British poetry, and sports and social issues.

Steinbeck grew up in the agriculturally rich Salinas Valley of central California, and although his family owned land, they were poor. Astro observes in the following selection that many of the settings and characters of Steinbeck's works are based on experiences in his youth and the continuing affinity for the residents and geography of that area of California. His writing and choice of subject matter, says Astro, often reveals his compassion for ordinary, beleaguered people and his disdain for materialism and middle-class values. While some critics believe that his writing and characterizations are overly sentimentalized, other scholars laud his ability to create sympathetic characters with whom readers can identify.

Steinbeck was born and grew up in that long, narrow strip of agricultural land called the Salinas Valley, which is bordered on the east by the Gabilon Mountains, on the west by the Santa Lucia range, and then Monterey Bay. He was the third of four children, and the only son, of John Ernst Steinbeck II, manager of a flour mill and treasurer of Monterey County, and Olive Hamilton Steinbeck, a former teacher. Years later Steinbeck said of his youth, "We were poor people with a hell of a lot of land which made us think we were rich people, even when we couldn't buy food and were patched." As a boy he explored the valley, following the Salinas River to its mouth in Monterey Bay and visiting the towns along its shore: Monterey, Carmel, Seaside, and Pacific Grove. He loved the Corral de Tierra and was awed by Big Sur, with its sea cliffs and forests.

In the Salinas Valley, in the Corral de Tierra, and on the Monterey Peninsula and Big Sur Steinbeck found much of the material for his fiction. *Of Mice and Men, In Dubious Battle,* and *The Grapes of Wrath,* as well as many of the stories in *The Long Valley,* are set in California's agricultural valleys. The action in *Tortilla Flat, Cannery Row,* and *Sweet Thursday* takes place along the waterfront of Monterey Bay. *The Pastures of Heaven* is Steinbeck's name for the Corral de Tierra. And the mystic quality of *To a God Unknown* owes much to the strange brooding nature of Big Sur. Later in life, Steinbeck became a New Yorker, and he summered in Sag Harbor rather than in Pacific Grove. Still, central California remained to Steinbeck what Yoknapatawpha was to [American author William] Faulkner. There is an acute consciousness of place in Steinbeck's California fiction, a way of seeing which informs the thematic design of his most successful work.

Steinbeck's College Years

Graduating from Salinas High School in 1919, Steinbeck entered Stanford University, which he attended intermittently until 1925. He had to work to pay for his education and sometimes took off one quarter to earn enough money to pay for the next quarter. He clerked in stores, worked as a surveyor in Big Sur, and was a hand on a ranch near King City, which he later used as the setting for *Of Mice and Men.* Several times he worked for the Spreckels Sugar Company, gaining firsthand knowledge of the labor problems he would write about in his political novels, *In Dubious Battle* and *The Grapes of Wrath.*

During the summer of 1923, Steinbeck took the general biology course at the Hopkins Marine Station in Pacific Grove, following an interest in marine biology that would be further stimulated in 1930 when he met marine biologist Edward F. Ricketts, whose ideas about the interrelationship of all life were to have a major impact on Steinbeck's world view, although Ricketts and Steinbeck had differing opinions on some points.

Steinbeck wrote fiction at Stanford, and in 1924 two of his stories appeared in the Stanford *Spectator*. After he left Stanford in June 1925, he worked his way to New York on a freighter through the Panama Canal. In New York he worked as a laborer until his uncle, Joseph Hamilton, found him a job on the *New York American*. Before long the newspaper fired him, and, discouraged by his inability to sell any of the stories he had been writing, he worked his way back to California on another freighter. He worked at a series of odd jobs in the Lake Tahoe area for the next two years and continued writing. In February 1928 he wrote to a friend that he had finished *Cup of Gold*, his first novel, but that he was already dissatisfied with it.

Steinbeck's First Novel Is Published

During the summer of 1928 Steinbeck met Carol Henning, whom he would marry in 1930, and later in 1928 he moved to San Francisco, where she had a job. Steinbeck shared an apartment with a friend and began work on a novel, which, after it had been rewritten several times and had several title changes, was published in 1933 as *To a God Unknown*.

In January 1929 Steinbeck received a telegram from Amassa Miller, a friend in New York who had been acting as Steinbeck's unofficial agent, informing him that Robert M. McBride and Company had accepted *Cup of Gold*. It had previously been rejected by seven other publishers.

Steinbeck's reaction to the book's publication was ambivalent. In late 1929 he wrote to a friend that the novel's sale "pays enough for me to live quietly and with a good deal of comfort. In that far it was worth selling," and to another friend he wrote, "The book was an immature experiment written for the purpose of getting all the wise cracks . . . and all the autobiographical material . . . out of my system. And I really did not intend to publish it. . . . I have not the slightest desire to step into Donn Byrne's shoes. I may not have his ability with the vernacular but I have twice his head. I think I have swept all the Cabellyo-Byrneish preciousness out for good." By 1932 he stated frankly, "I've outgrown it and it embarrasses me." . . .

In 1930 Steinbeck had met Edward F. Ricketts, who owned and operated the Pacific Biological Laboratory on the Monterey waterfront. At that time, Ricketts was already an accomplished scientist at work on the most complete and useful guide to the marine invertebrates of the central Pacific Coast ever written. He was an ecologist long before the study of interrelationships, of the mutuality of life forms, became a national interest. He was also a philosopher, a student of music and literature, and an essayist who studied not isolated things but the structure of relations. He dismissed as useless those "picklers of the field who see the pieces of life without its principle." . . .

Compassion for Ordinary People

Throughout *The Pastures of Heaven* [Steinbeck's second published novel], Steinbeck shows compassion, even affection, for the plight of ordinary people who strive for but cannot achieve happiness. Steinbeck never condemns their innocence, their simplicity, from the standpoint of middle-class values, but he portrays their self-destructive tendencies toward illusion and self-deception. *The Pastures of Heaven* is an ironic novel because in it Steinbeck shows us that however lovely or however redemptive the pastures of heaven may seem, true heaven cannot be attained by men on this earth.

Among Steinbeck's finest fictional creations are his primitives or half-wits and his escapees or his dropouts. Tularecito is his first half-wit, Junius Maltby his first escapee. Many others would follow. These simple people act as foils against which he can measure the excesses and eccentricities of material society. Steinbeck draws his primitives and his dropouts with great warmth. He admires their ability to live simply and easily, but he simultaneously depicts their inability to survive in the modern world. In diverse ways, they are either destroyed or driven back to the society from which they fled. . . .

Steinbeck Remarries and Has Two Sons

In the spring of 1941 Steinbeck and Carol Steinbeck separated, and in the fall Steinbeck moved to the East with Gwendolyn Conger (who soon changed the spelling of her first name to *Gwyndolyn*), a professional singer he had met the previous year. They lived for a time in the New York City area until Steinbeck went to Europe as a war correspondent for the *New York Herald Tribune* in 1943. Steinbeck was divorced from his first wife in 1942, and married Gwyndolyn Conger in 1943. They had two sons: Thom, born in August 1944, and John, born in June 1946. During the 1940s they lived at various times in New York and California. Steinbeck and Gwyndolyn Steinbeck separated and were divorced in 1948. . . .

The Seeds Are Sown for *The Pearl*

Shortly before he began work on *The Wayward Bus*, Steinbeck wrote a short piece based on a story he originally heard during his expedition to the Gulf of California. This was the story about a Mexican boy who found a great pearl which he thought would guarantee him happiness, but which almost destroyed him before he wisely threw it back into the sea. Steinbeck rewrote this fable a number of times, and when it was finally published in 1947 as *The Pearl*, it went largely unnoticed. It was not, in fact, until 1953 that Steinbeck discovered that it was at last "gathering some friends."

In contrast to the raucous bawdiness of *Cannery Row* and the allegorical seriousness of *The Wayward Bus*, *The Pearl* is a simple, lyrical fable which Steinbeck called "a black and white story like a parable." In this story of man's search for happiness and his need to choose between simplicity and complication, between a life in nature and a life in society, Steinbeck shows that the drive for wealth and power ends in tragedy and disappointment. *The Pearl* presents the human dilemma; it is the study of the agony involved in man's recognition of the vanity of human wishes. Kino, Steinbeck's protagonist, finds his pearl and protects it from those who would steal it from him, but he pays dearly. His house and canoe are destroyed and his child is killed. He comes to see the pearl as a gray, malignant growth, and so throws it back into the gulf. In doing so, Kino chooses what Ed Ricketts once called "the region of inward adjustments" (characterized by friendship, tolerance, dignity, and love) over "the region of outward possessions."

A Loss of Vision

Steinbeck's early postwar fiction reflects the vision of a man who had returned from a destructive war to a changed America. Trying first to recapture a sense of the past in *Cannery Row*, Steinbeck came to realize that neither the vagrant nor the scientific visionary could survive the onslaught of civilization. Then in *The Wayward Bus*, he focused directly on the people of that postwar world and attempted with little artistic success to depict their repentance. And finally, in *The Pearl* he employed legend to explain what he regarded as the greatest of human dilemmas. In these books, Steinbeck's organismal view of life, his belief that men can work together to fashion a better, more productive, and more meaningful life,

John Steinbeck is featured on a mural in Salinas, California, which was his boyhood home and which influenced many of the settings and characters found in his work. © Jamie Pham / Alamy.

seemed less and less applicable to the world he saw around him. Gradually, John Steinbeck was becoming a novelist without a vision. . . .

Death of Ricketts Deeply Affects Steinbeck

Steinbeck made preparations to join Ed Ricketts for another [specimen] collecting trip, this time to the west coast of Vancouver Island and the Queen Charlottes, for the purpose of writing a cold-water [version of his] *Sea of Cortez*. Steinbeck had never regretted collaborating with Ricketts on the Gulf of California narrative, but he recognized the inherent liabilities of any collaborative endeavor. In 1951, he told his editor, Pascal Covici, that "there are no good collaborations." Yet he had continued to show interest in Ricketts's work by writing the foreword to the second edition (1948) of Ricketts and Jack Calvin's *Between Pacific Tides*, and while he was already making preparations for work on "a giant novel" tentatively titled "Salinas Valley," he looked forward to another collaboration with Ricketts. But the marine biologist was killed in a freakish car/train wreck just weeks before the trip was to begin. Steinbeck was shattered by Ricketts's death. Later, he spoke of having had a kind of conscience removed and of possessing a new fierceness he had not felt for many years. But it is significant that he wrote little of consequence after Ricketts's death. As Jack Calvin has noted so succinctly, "The fountain had been turned off. Obviously, since he went on to write things like *Travels With Charley*, John was not aware that the train that killed Ed had also killed him as a writer." Steinbeck would spend the next several years wrestling in his writing with the fact of his own literary indebtedness to Ricketts. Throughout this period he continued to work on "Salinas Valley," which he finally completed in 1951 and retitled *East of Eden*, but his other writings between Ricketts's death in May of 1948 and the 1954 publication of *Sweet Thursday* reflect a rekindled absorption with Ricketts's person and idea.

In 1949, the recently divorced Steinbeck met and fell in love with Elaine Scott, then the wife of actor Zachary Scott. She became his third and last wife in December 1950. They lived mostly in and around New York City, and in 1955 when the Steinbecks bought a summer cottage in Sag Harbor, on eastern Long Island, it marked his decision to make the East Coast his permanent home. These changes, as well as his reaction to the death of Ricketts, suggest that the period between 1948 and 1955 was a period of reevaluation for Steinbeck....

Steinbeck Loses Interest in Writing Fiction

Steinbeck's final novel is *The Winter of Our Discontent* (1961), a book set in the fictional eastern Long Island community of New Baytown, which is above all a vision of the modern wasteland, a piercing study of the moral vacuum in contemporary America. In it, Steinbeck chronicles man's fall from grace as a result of his devotion to the all-holy dollar; all codes of individual and group morality have been replaced by a subservience to a fast-buck philosophy. . . .

There is evidence which suggests that by the time Steinbeck finished *The Winter of Our Discontent,* he had lost interest in writing fiction, and in his last years he was more active as a journalist and traveler than as a novelist. . . .

Steinbeck died in December of 1968. At the time of his death he was in critical disrepute, and there were few serious scholars who did not share Harry T. Moore's feeling that in the future Steinbeck's literary status would be that of a Louis Bromfield or a Bess Streeter Aldrich [considered as middlebrow or mawkish]. But the years have proved Moore wrong. Important new books, articles, and conferences about his work have made it clear that Steinbeck was a major American writer who defined well the human experience.

Steinbeck's Depictions of Mexicans Were Based on His Personal Experiences

Susan Shillinglaw

Susan Shillinglaw has been a professor of English at San Jose State University since 1984. She is also a scholar in residence at the National Steinbeck Center in Salinas, California. She has served as director of the Center for Steinbeck Studies at San Jose State University and editor of Steinbeck Studies. *Shillinglaw has many publications about John Steinbeck to her credit, including the 2006 volume* A Journey into Steinbeck's California.

Shillinglaw notes in the following selection that Steinbeck wrote frequently about Mexican subjects or Mexico itself. In fact, fully one-third of his work revolves around those subjects. The Mexican culture appealed to him because its people lived outside what he considered rigid middle-class morality. Steinbeck saw the American dream in different terms, tainted by an undercurrent of racial tension and violence. Shillinglaw believes that Steinbeck's stories involving Mexico and Mexicans demonstrate his sensitivity to their presence as part of the Western milieu. While Steinbeck was accused of portraying Mexicans as exotic and strange, Shillinglaw contends that even his critics must acknowledge his sympathetic portrayals of their struggles as outsiders.

A reconsideration is surely in order for [John Steinbeck], who wrote so frequently and searingly about race and ethnicity. One third of his work either is set in Mexico or treats Mexican subjects. And it is of no small significance that

Susan Shillinglaw, "Steinbeck and Ethnicity," *After the "Grapes of Wrath": Essays on John Steinbeck in Honor of Tetsumaro Hayashi*, Athens: Ohio University Press, 1995, pp. 41–44, 47. Copyright © 1995 by Ohio University Press. All rights reserved. Reproduced by permission.

his first published story—"Fingers of Cloud," which ran in *The Stanford Spectator* in 1924—treats an ethnic confrontation and his last published book—*America and Americans*—begins with a chapter on race in America. In that late text he writes: "From the first we have treated our minorities abominably, the way the old boys do the new kids in school. All that was required to release this mechanism of oppression and sadism was that the newcomers be meek, poor, weak in numbers, and unprotected . . . ". That statement holds one key to Steinbeck's concern with this country's attitude toward ethnics, for since childhood he had abhorred bullies and developed a quick sympathy for outcasts: a handicapped neighbor, foreign laborers. He visited often and spoke Spanish at the Wagners, a Salinas family that had lived in Mexico for three years. Throughout high school and college he worked with Mexicans at the Spreckels sugar plant and on the company's vast farms, hearing stories, sharing jokes. When he finally had a substantial advance from his publisher, his first trip with Carol Steinbeck in 1935 was a three-month stay in Mexico, a country he had long wished to visit and one to which he repeatedly returned.

Living Outside Middle-Class Culture

In short, he wrote about Mexican-Americans, in particular, because they, like his weary dreamers and gritty laborers, lived outside the dominant culture. He wrote about them because the energy and joy of their culture cut against the rigid middle-class morality that he long scorned, and because their lives and values critiqued the prevailing cultural mythos. As California writer and critic Gerald Haslam has noted, Steinbeck must be recognized for seeing the diversity of the state's population, for writing about the paisanos of Monterey, for example, at a time when the majority of Californians did not acknowledge the importance or even the existence of mixed-blood Mexicans. Not only did Steinbeck create a voice for these paisanos, but he also invoked prevailing patterns of the American mythos in giving them form.

Another statement made in the introductory essay in *America and Americans* suggests a second reason for Steinbeck's abiding interest in ethnicity. He tells a story about a native American he met when working at Lake Tahoe in the late 1920s:

> Many white people, after association with the tribesmen, have been struck with the dual life—the reality and super-reality—that the Indians seem to be able to penetrate at will. The stories of travelers in the early days are filled with these incidents of another life separated from this one by a penetrable veil; and such is the power of the Indians' belief in this other life that the traveler usually comes out believing in it too and only fearing that he won't be believed.

Compare this vision with one of Steinbeck's own, outlined in a 1930 letter to his Stanford classmate Carl Wilhelmson:

> Modern sanity and religion are a curious delusion. Yesterday I went out in a fishing boat—out in the ocean. By looking over the side into the blue water, I could quite easily see the shell of the turtle who supports the world. I am getting more prone to madness. What a ridiculous letter this is; full of vaguenesses and unrealities. I for one and you to some extent have a great many of the basic impulses of an African witch doctor.

The playful tone masks the letter's real significance. Steinbeck was no mere realist, either in art or life. Metaphysics intrigued him. Although many of his works have a realistic texture, a journalistic precision, they also contain layers of meaning beneath the surface, a point he often noted in correspondence when he referred to the various "levels" of his books. . . . Steinbeck was in large part attracted to "others" because of their exoticism and mysticism. A key question, of course, is whether or not he diminishes them by his treatment or if, as symbol or prophet or seer, these ethnics help blend ritual and realism, and thus help reconstruct a vision of wholeness.

Far from exhaustive, this essay will examine representative and sometimes problematic texts about the ethnic presence in America. It will focus on two strains plucked from *America and Americans*: first, Steinbeck's treatment of ethnicity as cultural saga; second, his fascination with the primitive as intriguing and often unfathomable other. . . .

America's Story Often Overlooks Ethnic Tensions

For embedded both in the American experience and in Steinbeck's retelling of the nation's Edenic impulse are other stories, ones of racial conflict, sexual excesses, tainted deeds. "Fingers of Cloud" articulates boldly—and with no little artistic uncertainty as to exactly what the 22-year-old author wanted to say—that America's story includes, but often suppresses, ethnic confrontations. For Steinbeck, the saga of continental conquest in broad sweep is a tale of Edenic expectation and consequent disillusionment; and that inevitable fall means, in part, that character and (more insistently) reader glimpse what so often taints the dream: racial and ethnic suppression and violence. . . .

That parable of America's dark destiny represents a defining moment in much of Steinbeck's fiction. Repeatedly he undercuts sagas of idealism, dynastic control, or social harmony with less insistent voices and stories of racial and ethnic turmoil. . . .

Steinbeck Casts Light on Minority Cultures

In short, throughout Steinbeck's work, fragmentary voices of ethnic Americans suggest, like an insistent discordant note, America's violent and oppressive past. Sexuality and violence are implosive in these texts. The stories and episodes convey, I think, not Steinbeck's racism—far from that—but rather his sensitivity to the contradictions at the heart of the American character and experience. Idealism, superficial structures of belief, confidence in American pragmatism, Edenic quests—all are altered or destroyed when touched by subversive violence, repressed knowledge, sexual energy.

More can be said, however, about Steinbeck's sensitivity to the ethnic presence in the West. Tales of California's settlement repeatedly show how intertwined are dominant and marginal voices. In each of his western epics—*To a God Unknown, The Grapes of Wrath,* and *East of Eden*—the patriarch is dethroned, his ties to the land severed, and family bonds strained. With the loss of certainty in cultural and familial coherence, voices other than those of the dominant culture emerge and carry the burden of meaning in each text....

Misguided Notions of a Patriarchal Society

Steinbeck has been accused of creating one-dimensional female characters as often as he has been said to create ethnic stereotypes. Both charges, I would argue, must be qualified by the thematic and cultural significance given alternative perspectives, both female and ethnic. That vision is, in many texts, only haltingly and belatedly acknowledged by central male characters who cannot abandon inherited notions of patriarchal control of family, fate and nature. But the very fragmentation of women and ethnics is precisely the point. Steinbeck's patriarchs cannot heed the words appealing to contractual bonds and readers often discount their import....

If, in part, Steinbeck's ethnic characters play key roles in his settlement dramas, they also enact significant parts in a personal and writerly drama. He cast himself early on as an outsider, and for much of his life he identified with marginal groups. His most sympathetic characters don't belong.

With other modernists, Steinbeck found in the untutored a vital source of artistic expression. Throughout his career

Mexican subjects in particular intrigued him because he identified with their otherness—a zest for life, scorn for a dominant culture, and an inherent exoticism and often mysticism. . . .

He kept returning to Mexico and Mexican subjects as a way to live and he translated that personal need into a cultural need.

Steinbeck Infused a Simple Parable with His Own Technique and Philosophy

Peter Lisca

Peter Lisca is a literary critic who has written extensively about the life and works of John Steinbeck.

Steinbeck made significant changes to a parable to align the story with his own goals and philosophy. In the following essay, Lisca asserts that Steinbeck's changes added levels of complexity and symbolism to the previously simple tale, transforming it into an adventure. His seemingly forthright prose adds dimension and meaning. Further, the third-person narration, often describing symbolic action, offers vivid descriptions that establish setting and convey the themes Steinbeck wanted to stress. Lisca adds that Steinbeck also interwove his view of the interrelatedness of nature throughout the story, a theme that appears in many of his fiction works.

The essential story had been in Steinbeck's mind since before the war. In *Sea of Cortez*, while remarking on the role of La Paz in providing the conquistadores with pearls, Steinbeck tells of an event "which happened at La Paz in recent years."

> An Indian boy by accident found a pearl of great size, an unbelievable pearl. He knew its value was so great that he need never work again.... In his great pearl lay salvation, for he could in advance purchase masses sufficient to pop him out of Purgatory like a squeezed watermelon seed.... He took his pearl to a broker and was offered so little that

Peter Lisca, "The Pearl," *The Wide World of John Steinbeck*, New Brunswick, NJ: Rutgers University Press, 1958, pp. 218–230. Copyright © 1958 by Rutgers, the State University. Reprinted by permission of Rutgers University Press.

he grew angry for he knew he was cheated. Then he carried his pearl to another broker and was offered the same amount. After a few more visits he came to know that the brokers were only the many hands of one head and that he could not sell his pearl for more. He took it to the beach and hid it under a stone, and that night he was clubbed into unconsciousness and his clothing was searched. The next night he slept at the house of a friend and his friend and he were injured and bound and the whole house searched. Then he went inland to lose his pursuers and he was waylaid and tortured. But he was very angry now and he knew what he must do. Hurt as he was he crept back to La Paz in the night and he skulked like a hunted fox to the beach and took out his pearl from under the stone. Then he cursed it and threw it as far as he could into the channel. He was a free man again with his soul in danger and his food and shelter insecure. And he laughed a great deal about it.

Steinbeck Made Changes to the Original Parable

When Steinbeck came to write "The Pearl of the World" four years later, he kept the basic pattern of this story—the discovery of the pearl, the persecution, and the renunciation—but he introduced certain important changes. The Indian boy becomes the man Kino, husband of Juana and father to Coyotito. The pearl is to provide not "the ability to be drunk as long as he wished," but an education for Coyotito: "My son will read and open books, and my son will write and will know writing. And my son will make numbers, and these things will make us free because he will know—he will know and through him we will know." The pearl is returned to the sea, but not before it has brought strife between husband and wife, destroyed their home, and caused the violent death of their child. Steinbeck also added several minor figures—a greedy doctor, a kind and understanding brother.

These changes were intended to amplify and make more complex those qualities of parable which Steinbeck perceived in the original. . . .

Physical Events Have a Deeper Meaning

Part of Steinbeck's success in creating this feeling in *The Pearl* lies in the theme itself. The action is simple, but, as in all parables, suggestive of underlying planes of meaning. The surface story is told in a manner which urges the reader to look beyond the physical events into their spiritual significance. . . .

In the story itself there are several details which suggest the symbolic nature of this pattern of events. When Kino first finds the pearl, it is described as "the greatest pearl in the world," and two pages later as "the Pearl of the World," a phrase which is often repeated. After the first attack on Kino by unknown assailants, his wife Juana says of the pearl, "This thing is evil. This pearl is like sin! It will destroy us. Throw it away, Kino. Let us break it between stones. Let us bury it and forget the place. Let us throw it back in the sea. It has brought evil. Kino, my husband, it will destroy us." But Kino's "face is set." The pearl has "cozened his brain with its beauty." The people of the village are suspicious. "That good wife Juana," they say, "and the beautiful baby Coyotito, and the others to come. What a pity it would be if the pearl should destroy them all." After Kino has insulted the agents who told him that the pearl was of no great value, his brother, Juan Tomás, says to him, "You have defied not the pearl buyers, but the whole structure, the whole way of life, and I am afraid for you." After the second attack on him, Kino still refuses to give up the pearl and says, "This pearl has become my soul. If I give it up I shall lose my soul."

This aura of suggestion extends not only to the pearl itself, but to the characters and setting as well. . . .

The Setting Also Suggests the Theme

The setting of *The Pearl* is just as suggestive as the theme, the characters, and the pearl itself: "The uncertain air that magnified some things and blotted out others hung over the whole Gulf so that all sights were unreal and vision could not be trusted; so that sea and land had the sharp clarities and the vagueness of a dream.... Part of the far shore disappeared into a shimmer that looked like water. There was no certainty in seeing, no proof that what you saw was there or was not there."

When Kino and Juana escape from their coastal village, they "go out into the world." At one point in their flight, the landscape, though realistically described, has the same symbolic suggestiveness that the landscape has in [Steinbeck's short stories] "Flight" and "The Great Mountains":

> The land was waterless, furred with the cacti which could store water and with the great-rooted brush which could reach deep into the earth for a little moisture and get along on very little. And underfoot was not soil but broken rock, split into cubes, great slabs, but none of it water-rounded. Little tufts of sad dry grass grew between the stones, grass that had sprouted with a single rain and headed, dropped its seed, and died. Horned toads watched the family go by and turned their little pivoting dragon heads.... The stinging heat lay over this desert country, and ahead the stone mountains looked cool and welcoming....

Steinbeck Makes the Parable an Adventure

However meaningful the parable of the pearl may be in the abstract, Steinbeck's success in fleshing out this parable to the dimensions of a credible, forceful human adventure ultimately rests on his prose style, which is flexible to the extent that here as in most of his other novels it becomes technique as well as medium. It is capable not only of creating an aura of symbolic suggestion (as in the descriptions of landscape cited above), but also of rendering details in terms of a camera—as when Kino, in hiding, peers at his pursuers:

> Kino could see only their legs and only the legs of the horse from under the fallen branch. He saw the dark horny feet of the men and their ragged white clothes, and he heard the creak of leather of the saddle and the clink of spurs. The trackers stopped at the swept place and studied it, and the horseman stopped. The horse flung his head up against the bit and the bit-roller clicked under his tongue and the horse snorted. Then the dark trackers turned and studied the horse and watched his ears.

The more panoramic descriptions have this same reality and authenticity, which create a firm foundation for the abstract pattern:

> The beach was yellow sand, but at the water's edge a rubble of shell and algae took its place. Fiddler crabs bubbled and sputtered in their holes in the sand, and in the shallows little lobsters popped in and out of their tiny homes in the rubble and sand. The sea bottom was rich with crawling and swimming and growing things. The brown algae waved in the gentle currents and the green eel grass swayed and little sea horses clung to its stems. Spotted botete, the poison fish, lay on the bottom in the eel-grass beds, and the bright-colored swimming crabs scampered over them.

Characters Are Portrayed Objectively

The objectivity of the prose style in these descriptive passages is paralleled by Steinbeck's objectivity in portraying his characters' inner feelings. The pearl buyer's nervousness while he is waiting for Kino to walk up the street and into his office is conveyed by a nervous tic which is at the same time a perfect visual symbol of his legerdemain [deception or trickery] activities as a pearl buyer: "He rolled a coin back and forth over his knuckles and made it appear and disappear, made it

John Steinbeck, seen here in an undated photo, often wrote of characters who struggle on the margins of society. © AP Images.

spin and sparkle. The coin winked into sight and as quickly slipped out of sight, and the man did not even watch his own performance." . . .

Symbolic Actions Replace Narration

A more complex example of this substitution of symbolic action for omniscient narration is the action with which the novel ends. After Coyotito is killed, Kino and Juana come back to their village and walk wordlessly through the crowded streets. "The sun was behind them and their long shadows stalked ahead, and they seemed to carry two towers of darkness with them." They do not pause until they come to the shore.

> And then Kino laid the rifle down, and he dug among his clothes, and then he held the great pearl in his hand. . . . Kino's hand shook a little, and he turned slowly to Juana and held the pearl out to her. She stood beside him, still holding her dead bundle over her shoulder. She looked at the pearl in his hand for a moment and then she looked into Kino's eyes and said softly, "No, you."

> And Kino drew back his arm and flung the pearl with all his might. Kino and Juana watched it go, winking and glimmering under the setting sun. They saw the little splash in the distance, and they stood side by side watching the place for a long time.

For the reader who has been following the story, these bare details are rich with unstated meaning. . . .

Steinbeck Incorporates His View of Nature

The Pearl brings together several more of Steinbeck's techniques and preoccupations as a writer. His tendency to think of groups as unit animals is revealed in his description of the "nerve lines" and "units" of a small town. His non-teleological thinking [i.e., that things do not necessarily have a goal or purpose] and his unwillingness to assign absolute blame and create "villains" is evident here as in *In Dubious Battle, The Grapes of Wrath, The Moon Is Down*, and *Sea of Cortez*. The pearl buyers' motives in attempting to cheat Kino are understood. Like the "owners" of *In Dubious Battle* and *The Grapes of Wrath*, they are but part of a system, "and if it be a man's function to break down a price, then he must take joy and satisfaction in breaking it as far down as possible. For every man in the world functions to the best of his ability, and no one does less than his best, no matter what he may think about it."

There is also in *The Pearl* Steinbeck's technique of interrupting the action to insert a passage illustrating predatory nature as an implicit comment on that action. After the doctor has learned of Kino's great pearl and has come on a professional visit he has previously refused to make, there occurs the following description, set off as a separate paragraph: "Out in the estuary a tight woven school of small fishes glittered and broke water to escape a school of great fishes that drove in to eat them. And in the houses the people could hear the swish of the small ones and the bouncing splash of the great ones as the slaughter went on. . . . And the night mice crept about on the ground and the little night hawks hunted them silently." This and similar passages throughout Steinbeck's works serve not to suggest that nature is evil, but to remind man of his continuity with nature, and to reveal the predatory drive which, beneath his civilized mask, he shares with other living creatures.

Social Issues
in Literature

CHAPTER 2

The Pearl and Poverty

The Pearl Initially Separates Kino from His Simple Life

Tetsumaro Hayashi

Tetsumaro Hayashi, an emeritus professor of English at Ball State University in Indiana, is a highly regarded and extensively published Steinbeck scholar. He served as director of the Steinbeck Research Institute at Ball State for twenty-three years. Hayashi also was president of the International Steinbeck Society from 1980 to 1994.

In the following selection Hayashi's analysis focuses on the view that The Pearl *operates on two levels: Kino's withdrawal from all that his family and society mean to him as an individual, and his subsequent realization that the pearl symbolizes the greed of others. At first, Kino imagines the pearl as the great equalizer with those of greater wealth. Hayashi relies on terms from Zen philosophy to illustrate the theme of total disengagement, the act of Kino letting go of the false promise of the pearl. When Kino loses his real "pearl," his son, he finally awakens to the true evil of the pearl.*

John Steinbeck's *The Pearl* can properly be called the novel of disengagement on at least two levels, for it traces the symbolic journey and withdrawal of the novel's protagonist, Kino, first from the environment of society, his family, and even from his own proper place in the natural scheme; and, secondly, from the charm of the Pearl of the World. The first withdrawal is best seen as the misguided alienation from everything that gives life spiritual value and moral direction; the second is best seen as the recognition of the pearl as a symbol of the perverse greed inherent in the scheme of things which,

Tetsumaro Hayashi, "*The Pearl* as the Novel of Disengagement," *Steinbeck Quarterly*, Ball State University, vol. 2, nos. 3 and 4, Summer/Fall 1974, pp. 84–88. Copyright © 1974 by American Journal of Business. All rights reserved. Reproduced by permission.

like the scorpion's poison, can infect an otherwise healthy organism, such as Kino's being and that of his family.

Kino Accepts False Values

The novel operates on two levels, then, and draws its dynamic flow from a recurrent process of commitment to false values and a later disengagement from them. The pearl, thus, is not the means to freedom, with its promises of wealth, pride, respect, status, and hope for his family, in reality it is a self-discovered poison and the visible symbol not of material poverty, but of moral bankruptcy, not of salvation but of the inherent "heart of darkness" dormant in every human breast. It takes *Gedatsu* [total disengagement or extrication in Zen philosophy], the total disengagement from this magnificent obsession, to save him from the curse of the Pearl of the World. The face of evil, here and everywhere, is at first brilliant, attractive, and tempting. It is only natural, then, that when Kino first discovers the pearl, he is deceived by its brilliance and the false promise it holds out to him. His fascination with the pearl becomes so great, in fact, that it soon becomes his total obsession, completely upsetting his scale of values, displacing his sense of filial and social community, and even consuming his moral sense. Thus he declares that "This pearl has become my soul. If I give it up, I shall lose my soul." An obsessed man, Kino embraces false values and equates the symbol of material wealth with the soul.

Kino Becomes Obsessed with the Pearl

Kino's faith in the seemingly desirable nature of the pearl is no less than an obsession, an obsession made with almost religious fervor, as the pearl becomes Kino's new God. This allegorical shift is expressed by Steinbeck's favorite device, namely, the literary "montage" which gives the reader a dual image of the pearl as a thematic focus. It is still true, nevertheless, that the pearl is at one point Kino's dream of the future and his indulgence in an elevated new status in society. Yet the same object, so priceless and so beautiful, symbolizes a false sense of value that blinds Kino and so many other men and prompts them to become evil-minded, greedy, fearful, and destructive. The pearl buyers, the doctor, and their agents, become "slaves of passion," no doubt; but Kino joins their company in prizing what they value. The pearl, as a mammon [material wealth that has an evil or immoral influence], appears to be a "Life Force," and yet it is an allegory of Death. Therefore, the possessor of the pearl is in reality possessed by its charm; he is at once blessed and cursed, owner and slave, freed from poverty but chained to his enemies.

Kino Loses His Real Pearl, His Son

Ironically enough, the pearl is bound to destroy its possessor and all those who covet it. And yet Kino, like those who are enslaved by avarice, temporarily loses his spiritual vision until he loses his real "Pearl" in the world: his only son, Coyotito. Like Mr. Kurtz in Joseph Conrad's *Heart of Darkness*, whose soul is possessed by the ivory and his lust for it, Kino is possessed by the pearl and his obsession with it. And, lifeless God now has a mysterious dual image: the image of life and the simultaneous image of death. Kino does not fully recognize its duality until his son is shot to death by one of the pursuers. Then in the pearl can he clearly see the dual image: the "frantic eyes of the man (Kino killed) in the pool" and "Coyotito lying in the little cave with the top of his head shot away." Ironically, the name "Coyotito" means "little Coyote" in Spanish, and the boy is thus perhaps not only a son but a symbol of the living force in nature condemned to be the victim of the predatory instinct in man.

However, through his *Gedatsu*, Kino learns to face his Fate when he is chased by the invisible pursuers. When he is convinced that there is "no exit," he experiences Hamlet's *Satori* [awakening or illumination in Zen philosophy] as exemplified

Tetsumaro Hayashi states that when Kino loses his true pearl, his son, he reaches the Zen state of Satori, *the "Great Illumination."* © George Diebold / Blend Images / Corbis.

by the Prince's ultimate concerns: "The readiness is all" and "Let it be." Kino, like Prince Hamlet, recognizes that he would have to face his Fate sooner or later, and the only way to find the way from bondage to freedom is to confront Fate with courage and dignity. As Kino experiences this *Satori*, his Great Illumination, he is able to extricate himself from the self-discovered prison: the Pearl of the World, the false promise and deceptive mammon. . . .

Kino's Rejection of the Pearl Starts a War

As soon as Kino starts an underclared war against the absurd society of pearl buyers, the doctor, and their agents, the enemies immediately try to kill Kino and his family and to steal his pearl. Discovering the pearl, therefore, turns out to be like tasting the Forbidden Fruit. Like Adam and Eve, Kino and Juana have to be banished from the Eden-like society after they are exposed to the secret knowledge of evil through the Pearl of the World; ultimately, this proves to be a "Fortunate Fall," for Kino finally experiences his *Satori*. After his discovery there will continuously be a vicious circle around Kino; the more he protects the ownership of the pearl, the more exposed he is to the dangers of invisible enemies. Kino cannot find his peace of mind until he disengages himself totally from his magnificent obsession with the pearl, the very source that contaminates him. The pearl, like the evil king in the Elizabethan world who spiritually pollutes the kingdom, contaminates Kino's soul and attempts to destroy his tie with the village and nature where he, though poor, would find happiness, peace, harmony, and love.

Coyotito's Death Impels Kino's Awakening

However, Coyotito's death forces him to recognize the illusion he has taken as a reality; his son's sudden death is a kind of sacrifice to a pagan god Kino has blindly and fanatically worshipped; this painful experience restores Kino's sanity and vision. At long last Kino is able to recognize the naked truth: the pearl will never insure his future, but destroy it. He regains a kind of stability and vision that makes him recognize the truth, that the only way to be saved is to be without the pearl, without the obsession: specifically, it is through the equally magnificent *disengagement* from the mammon, that he can achieve his salvation. This means that a total self negation gives him subdued but enduring freedom from bondage and fear and that he now is able to face his future and to discover a new purpose in the otherwise "absurd and cruel" society. He has looked into the evil ... not only in others but in himself, and withdrawn from that confrontation with a darker being within himself; thus he becomes aware of the true nature of man and his lonely Fate.

It is this *Satori* that brings Kino and Juana back to their village; there is something inviolable about them when they quietly walk through the village. There is no fear, no obsession, no anger. By throwing the Pearl of the World back into the sea, Kino has regained his peace, security, and most importantly, his natural tie with the village. He is once again able to live there, not as an alienated figure, but as a citizen of his own community, which is his only reality. Paradoxically speaking, he restores his real being by totally renouncing his false being. Thus Steinbeck's *The Pearl*, the novel of disengagement, tells us the very painful but noteworthy journey of Kino's *Gedatsu* and *Satori*, which finally teaches him the way to bring himself from bondage to freedom, from fear to fearlessness, and from Death to Rebirth. He restores himself by means of his total self-negation.

Kino Initially Chooses Enslavement to Wealth to Escape Poverty

Sydney J. Krause

Sydney J. Krause is an emeritus professor of English at Kent State University in Ohio and a fellow in the university's Institute for Bibliography and Editing, which he founded in 1965. He has published articles and books on a variety of topics related to American literature.

According to Krause in the following essay, Kino's motives for coveting the pearl are no better than those of the upper-class town residents. He displaces his family and his values and sells out, thinking he can improve his life with the pearl. He becomes enslaved to the pearl, and his community becomes as enraptured by its possibilities as does Kino. Krause states that Kino finally realizes that continued possession of the pearl will cause a struggle for survival on a different basis. Kino redeems himself by rejecting the pearl and all that it stands for.

Kino is to be seen as sharing in the community feeling of self-satisfaction with things as they are before he becomes the victim of it. His future is in this manner socially fated even before fate and society intervene to specifically determine it, but once he has the pearl, the earlier subconscious identification with community feeling operates in an interestingly ironic pattern as Kino begins to size up the inverted value system by which the world operates. This occurs just after he has acquired the pearl and as—with his dreams full-blown—he thinks it can deliver him the world, a reflection that brings on

Sydney J. Krause, "*The Pearl* and "Hadleyburg": From Desire to Renunciation," *Steinbeck Quarterly*, Ball State University, vol. 7, no. 1, Winter 1974, pp. 9–12, 14. Copyright © 1974 by American Journal of Business. All rights reserved. Reproduced by permission.

his first glimmer of apprehension—*i.e.*, that he will have to protect himself from attack. The important factor here is that . . . Kino's motives are not a whit better than those of the respectable, oppressor class (greed, envy, pride, vengeance are already in evidence), and his culpability . . . , is also identical with that of his enemy, the upper-class community. Incredibly enough, the man is reading his own fate in its terms. Juana is at the hearth again and he feels "all warmth and security" on hearing the Song of the Family. But he sets aside its values, as, pearl in hand, he thinks about improving his material lot; and "by saying what his future was going to be like, he had created it." . . . Kino went into his temptation with open eyes and then closed them to what he knew: "that the gods do not love men's plans" and that they "take their revenge on a man if he be successful through his own efforts." . . . Morally, he chose another enslavement. That is exactly what Kino does; he exchanges one form of enslavement for another, and naturally the chosen one turns out to be worse.

Steinbeck was rather insistent on our seeing Kino's fall as both self-willed and determined by his attachment to establishment thinking (he is after all going to outwit the pearl buyers), for when Juan Tomás told him of the men who had been sent to the capital to get a fair price for the fishermen's pearls and had absconded with them, Kino held "it was against religion," and went on to say—in ironic prophecy—"The loss of the pearl was a punishment visited on those who tried to leave their station." . . .

Kino Sells His Respectability

Kino is no coward. He seems to have a stronger character. Yet if one examines his early actions carefully enough one detects certain irrational evasions. There is indeed something to what [literary critic Warren] French says about a "sell-out" to respectability; however, it is not at all Steinbeck's (he is obviously critical of it), but Kino's in his fallen state. In the rush to the town doctor, which became a "neighborhood affair," Kino anticipated the rejection even before it came. He felt "rage and terror" enough to want to kill the doctor, whose "race" had "for nearly four hundred years beaten and starved and robbed and despised Kino's race, and frightened it too." Yet, once at the gate, Kino humbly removes his hat; and when the expected insult comes, the whole "soft-footed procession" feels so thoroughly shamed, they must move away so that the "public shaming" Kino brought upon himself "will no longer be in their eyes". Then comes the Pearl of the World, and the humiliation is forgotten. One dream crowds out the other and we have the total sell-out. Kino wants all of the things valued by the town society that had just shamed him, so that—supposedly—he will never be shamed again.

The comparable sins of Kino's community are more obvious than his—but only to the reader. The community is publicly as oblivious to its inconsistency as Kino is to his. They regard the finding of the pearl as a "great marvel," an event "time would date from," but—just in case—they are also prepared to say "a foolish thing came over him" and that "God punished Kino because he rebelled against the way things are". As word spreads to the town, the priest thinks of church repairs, the shopkeepers look at the clothes they have not sold, the Doctor thinks of Paris, the beggars of alms-giving, the pearl buyers of the lowest price they think Kino will stand. "Kino's pearl went into the dreams, the speculations, the schemes . . . the hungers of everyone. . . . "

Kino Sees the Ugly Side of the Pearl

He too learns about the ugliness of cupidity by seeing it in others, and his initial thought that the community shared his joy also gives way to suspicion, so that while he cannot quite know the envy he has aroused (he suddenly became the one who "stood in the way" and was "every man's enemy") when Juana asks whom does he fear as he re-buries the pearl for the night, he does instinctively reply, "Everyone". It is in the air. Everyone knows it and no one admits it. . . .

Kino must be seen as *trying* to do the right thing; and, given his circumstances, he does not have many alternatives. When he decides he will go to the capital to sell his pearl, Juan Tomás tells him (in ironic echo of Kino's judgment on others who had tried it), "You have defied not the pearl buyers, but the whole structure, the whole way of life, and I am afraid for you". In spite of its having been general knowledge that "the nerves of the townspeople [would] ring with nervousness" if one man stepped out of the "known and trusted pattern", it was natural for Kino to resist the unpleasant truth when it was *he* who would be affected by it. . . . Although Kino saw he had "lost his old world," he still somehow reasoned it was merely the "chance" he wanted for his son that was being attacked and that the threat to him would be a threat to the entire brush hut community. "My friends will protect me," he says, to which Juan Tomás soberly rejoins, "Only so long as they are not in danger or discomfort from it". . . . What is interesting is how Steinbeck uses this commentary with his protagonist, as when he offsets Kino's genuine groping for knowledge of the right thing to do with the disillusioning fact that his own passion is the greatest obstacle to it. Thus at the apex of Kino's swollen cupidity, and while his aim still seems worthy. Steinbeck voices a typical [Mark] Twainian irony: "It is said that humans are never satisfied, that you give them one thing and they want something more. And this is said in disparagement, whereas it is one of the greatest talents the species has and one that has made it superior to animals that are satisfied with what they have".

Kino Faces the Issues of the Pearl's Evil

It is only after receiving physical evidence of the dark hostility around him, "the evil . . . all about," the beatings and the destruction of his canoe and home, and after Juana has pointed out that his having killed a man in self-defense will carry no weight with the townspeople ("Do you remember the men of the city? Do you think your explanation will help?"), that Kino finally abandons all illusions about his fellow man, and sees he must go it alone.

The issues are at last drawn with a full consciousness on Kino's part that, given the course he has chosen, continued possession of the pearl means a struggle for survival on somewhat other terms than those initially contemplated. There can of course be no self-enlightenment so long as he continues to ignore the fact that possession of the pearl will assure the very fate he is trying to avoid by retaining it. Capable as he proves himself to be physically in overcoming his pursuers, he has yet to grapple with the greater evil within. However, some progress has been made; for, from the tragic admission of one cold truth, "this pearl has become my soul" there soon follows another, "the music of the pearl had become sinister in his ears, and it was interwoven with the music of evil". But the worst truth of all remains unacknowledged: knowing this he still clings to hopes for all that the pearl may bring him in worldly goods. Indeed, he can read the vision of his error in the "shining surface" of the pearl itself (he looks for a vision of the rifle it will buy and instead sees the man he had killed; he contemplates the church wedding and instead sees Juana's beaten face; etc.) and yet be incapable of acting on what it tells him. . . .

Kino Recaptures His Honor and Values

If social alienation did not solve Kino's individual problem, it was the beginning of an important moral revelation. He could see that his regard for justice placed him on one side and the community on the other. . . .

So intense is the fear and hostility Kino and Juana arouse on their return that mothers turn their children's faces from

These Mexican coins were in circulation when The Pearl *was published. Kino's visions of wealth and desire for privilege threaten to destroy him.* © PjrStudio / Alamy.

them, and Juan Tomás cannot voice the feeble greeting which his "uncertainly" raised left hand attempts to convey.

Were the story to end there, it would amply fulfill the bleakest construction critics have placed on its outcome. But it does not. The climax is yet to come. Keenly aware of the tension surrounding him. Kino remains "immune." This display of strength of will is the direct result of his moral awakening. He has lost his son but reclaimed his soul. The mood of despair, then, is not something he himself gives in to; it is rather *a measure of all that he rises above*: "They had gone through pain and had come out on the other side". However much his story had been intertwined with that of the community and its values, he has at the end truly liberated himself from those values. His new freedom and immunity are his transcendence of them. He and Juana walk past the remains of their burned house and their broken canoe and look at neither. Symbolically, Kino lays down the rifle, brings out the pearl, which is now "ugly," "gray" and "malignant" and has "evil faces" peering from its surface; and then, his hand shaking, he holds it out to Juana to dispose of. By this dramatic public admission of personal wrong, the man has truly reclaimed his soul. He has earned the right to make the formal renunciation, which

Juana grants him. He has triumphed over the direst peril to achieve personal redemption. He is free. Nothing can touch him anymore.

This moral resolution of the story is not suddenly sprung at the end. On the contrary, it was rather carefully prepared for. Kino could not have redeemed himself were he not the proud man he had been at the outset. By a juxtaposing conversion of values that is a proper sequel to the one by which society's seeming good was disclosed to be actual evil, Kino's greatest weakness finally became his greatest strength.

The Townspeople in *The Pearl* Have a Parasitic Relationship with the Poor

Ernest E. Karsten Jr.

Ernest E. Karsten Jr. was a teacher at Castlemont High School in Oakland, California, when he wrote this essay in collaboration with a colleague, Gita S. Kornfeld.

In Karsten's view, voiced in the following article, the people of Kino's community live in harmony with one another in their houses made of brush, an element of nature, while the town is made of harder and less forgiving materials—plaster and stone. The town is an unnatural environment created by those descended from the conquistadores, the oppressors of Kino's people. Respect and responsibility for one another, says Karsten, are hallmarks of Kino's community. The townspeople take advantage of Kino and his people, acting as selfish predators. Karsten points out Steinbeck's imagery throughout the story to illustrate the parasitic relationship between the two groups of people.

Within the first few pages [of *The Pearl*], Steinbeck presents a pair of descriptive phrases which he will continue to use. . . . He juxtaposes the "brush houses" of the community and the "stone and plaster houses" of the town. This basic image suggests several ideas. Perhaps the first is the idea of impermanence on the one hand and solidity on the other. Life for the community is a precarious as well as a precious thing, subject not only to the whims of Fate but to the demands of the town, its needs and wants; the town, however, has the strength to withstand Chance and to endure.

Ernest E. Karsten Jr., "Thematic Structure in *The Pearl*," *English Journal*, vol. 54, no. 1, January 1965, pp. 1–7. Published by National Council of Teachers in English (NCTE).

The Town Is an Unnatural Existence

Steinbeck elaborates upon his description of the town. He progresses from the "stone and plaster houses" to the phrase "city of stone and plaster," and further to "the city of harsh outer walls and inner cool gardens where a little water played and the bougainvillaea crusted the walls with purple, brick-red, and white," and finally to "the secret gardens . . . the singing of caged birds . . . and the splash of cooling water on hot flagstones." Later he repeats the images by referring to the wall, water, and caged birds.

The images of the "secret gardens," "caged birds," and fountains bespeak verdant and cool beauty beneath a relentless sun. What could be more desirable? Or natural? Yet, if these images are suggestive of human relationships, of the juxtaposed modes of life, their normalcy must be questioned. Thus, as "stone and plaster houses" suggests a retreat from the vital contest, so too do these images suggest a refuge. Moreover, they are unnatural. A "secret garden" is the property of one who cannot appreciate nature's garden wherever it may be, primarily it would seem, because nature's garden is not his alone. Similarly, a "caged bird" is only a substitute for the melodies so naturally a part of Kino's people, and a fountain is a poor imitation of the lullaby of the sea. These images at first thought are completely acceptable; but, when questioned, they corroborate the picture of the town as protective and withdrawn from life and nature and suggest that the people are almost as lifeless and unnatural as their gardens.

The Town Has Erected Barriers

In the phrase, "harsh outer walls," Steinbeck not only reinforces the defensive ideas of retreat and refuge, but also suggests another idea—an offensive barrier against outsiders, the barrier of racial prejudice, from behind which the economic, social, and cultural oppression of the community by the town is advanced. But this barrier is callously camouflaged with bougainvillaea. Here too, however, the camouflage itself is descriptive of the town, for the blossoms of the bougainvillaea are symbolic in color: the purple can represent royalty or imperial rank, the *conquistadores* of the Spanish kings whose descendants are the oppressors of Kino's people, or it can symbolize the heinous sins of prejudice and avarice; brick-red can represent the extent of the hatred of the town for the community or, more likely, the blood that has been shed in the subjugation of the Indians; white, although it very often suggests innocence and purity, can also symbolize cowardice or can refer to the white vestments of the clergy, specifically the white cassock or surplice of some of the mendicant orders in early Mexico, and to the royalist, conservative, anti-Indian political viewpoint.

We have finally worked back to the key phrase, "city of stone and plaster," by which Steinbeck combines all that has been suggested about the town with what he will reveal in the nameless individuals of the town. "Stone" continues to represent endurance, strength, refuge, protection, coldness, and harshness; the image created by "plaster," however, is again that of camouflage, the shell-like mask worn by the town to conceal its parasitic reality.

A Parasitic Relationship

Even in what might be termed indirect description, Steinbeck has pictures of the parasitic relationship between the community and the town. In the first instance of metaphors from the animal world, Steinbeck reports how an ant, a social animal working for the good of its colony, has been trapped by an ant-lion, living near the ant colony to prey upon it for his individual needs. In the same way the individuals of the town have built "traps" to take advantage of the ignorance of the Indians and to prey upon them for whatever they have of wealth, labor, or services. Next the author cites the example of the hungry dogs and pigs of the town which scavenge the beach searching for dead fish or seabirds, the latter here representing the Indians who live off the sea and who for all general purposes are *dead* because they have no power to resist, while the former represent the greedy townspeople. In a third metaphor Steinbeck describes the fish that live near the oyster beds to feed off the rejected oysters and to nibble at the inner shells. Perhaps this is the most forceful of the metaphors, for the author seems to be saying that the Indians, the rejects of modern society, thrown back after having been despoiled of their wealth by that society, are the prey of the townspeople who live nearby and who scavenge even upon the hopes, dreams, and souls of these people. Finally in the metaphor of the large fish feeding on the small fish, Steinbeck supplies a simple restatement of this parasitic relationship between the town and the community, and perhaps a picture of the inevitability of such a relationship in nature.

In summation, then, let us return to that first pair of descriptive phrases for an inventory of the images therein before relating descriptions to the central theme. "Brush houses" suggests contact with the elements, with nature, with life. If there is a strenuous struggle for existence in the community, there is also exhilaration in the confrontation with nature that such dwellings make possible. In addition the possibility or desire for human contact is evident in the phrase, which suggests openness and a lack of any permanent barriers. In contrast, "stone and plaster houses" creates further the images of retreat from the vital contest into a protected passivity, of fear of elemental forces, of impregnable refuge from the uninvited, of aloof coldness.

Indians Represent Interdependence

In Kino's community all have a sense of responsibility to one another and a respect for the humanity of each. Coyotito's scream attracts the neighbors' sympathetic attention as well as curiosity, and the neighbors accompany Kino to the doctor's when the community makes one of its few incursions into the town. Upon the doctor's refusal to treat the child, the neighbors will not shame Kino and abandon him so that he will not have to face them. The discovery of the pearl brings them again, this time to share the joy and dreams; yet, they are more concerned for Kino than they are interested in the pearl. The neighbors again come to Kino when the doctor appears to inflict temporary illness upon Coyotito. They also go with Kino when he attempts to sell the pearl as a necessary sign of friendship; and both before and after the visit, Juan Tomas emerges from the group to represent the thinking of the community. During the crisis, Kino could escape; but he will not commit sacrilege against the community by taking another's boat. Although the neighbors demonstrate concern at the fire and grief over the supposed deaths of Kino and his family, Kino's relationship with the community has been destroyed because of the murder; and he must leave to protect the community and his brother ("I am like a leprosy.").

The Town Drains Life from the Community

The town, on the other hand, is like a separate organism, walled off from the life of the community, yet living only to drain off that life. With the beggars acting as seers for our benefit, the parasitic relationship becomes clear in the actions of three people of the town, unnamed as if they were really impersonal forces, yet singled out for individual roles. It is through them that one can see all the characteristics that Steinbeck's description has implied.

"The doctor will not come," say the neighbors; and when the child is taken to him, the doctor will not treat him. As a person, he is cold and withdrawn from the life around him; his only concern is his desire to return to France. He has his "secret garden," his bedroom, where his life is that of a wealthy French aristocrat. In his actions, the doctor depicts the harsh barriers of prejudice, from his first remarks in refusing to

According to Ernest E. Karsten Jr., the town's harsh outer wall of stone and plaster represents the townspeople's exclusion of the Indian population, which the bougainvillea vainly attempts to camouflage. © LeighSmithImages / Alamy.

treat Coyotito ("I am a doctor, not a veterinary.") to his apparently callous experiment with the boy, as if he were some laboratory animal. When the doctor puts on his friendly face, his plaster mask, after the pearl has been found, it is only to gain entree into Kino's hut. He has willingly emerged from behind the harsh barrier to use his knowledge and status to discover the pearl's hiding place and to try to steal it. Steinbeck makes us aware of this camouflage by saying that the doctor's purpose had been discerned by the people, for he "was not good at dissembling."

Another dissembler is the priest, whom the news of the pearl has brought probably for the first time in many months to see what part of the wealth he can get for the Church. When he addresses these "children," he makes the words "sound like a benediction." Yet, in the sermon that he gives annually, he associates himself with the town's oppression and strengthens its parasitic stranglehold upon the community by sanctifying it. Like the doctor, at the news of the pearl, the priest reacts selfishly and emerges from behind the protective wall to raid the sudden new wealth of the community.

The Predatory Pearl Buyers

It is the pearl buyer, however, who wins the prize for best masquerade—always joking, hand-shaking, calling out greetings, a friend and sympathizer to all, but ferret-eyed, masking all emotion behind a stone-walled face, concentrating the nervous energy inherent in the predatory quest of prey in the ceaselessly excited, always secret movements of a coin trick. In league with the other buyers, he tries to cheat Kino—the attack from behind the wall of economic oppression. Indeed, all the pearl buyers represent that wall, for as agents of a single man they stand together as the harsh barrier of monopoly. Yet, each one, since he appears to be an independent agent, acts as camouflage, as a camouflaging blossom hiding that wall. Realizing their failure to cheat Kino, they later try to rob him. Then, directly or indirectly, after Kino has determined to circumvent that wall of monopoly by selling his pearl elsewhere, they destroy all that Kino has of value, his boat and his home.

In general, the townspeople as presented in the novel suggest the characteristics of parasitism, especially the retreat from strenuous struggle, the passive mode of life. In addition, the pearl buyers, as agents of a single unnamed, never introduced individual, show another characteristic, that of retreat from independent endeavor. Finally, the doctor symbolizes the unmistakable degeneration that results from parasitism.

Kino and Juana Must Learn to Live in a World of Dualities

Michael J. Meyer

Michael J. Meyer, who died in March 2011, retired as an adjunct professor of English at DePaul University in Chicago. Meyer was a recognized Steinbeck scholar and had served on the editorial board of the Steinbeck Quarterly. *His literary criticism was published in the* Steinbeck Review, *as well as in other publications. He also published two Steinbeck bibliographies.*

Meyer proposes in the following selection that Kino and Juana undergo an initiation into the world and lose their naive view of society. They struggle to come to terms with a new reality that includes both good and evil. The images of light and dark, harmony and dissonance, pervade their experience after the pearl enters their lives. Still, says Meyer, Kino and Juana want to ignore the duality they confront, motivated by the success they envision for themselves. Kino eventually realizes the darkness is like the evil side of the pearl but continues to lack understanding of the duality of their world. Juana, however, is the first to comprehend the darkness the pearl has brought to their lives.

Steinbeck asserts that duality undergirds all of man's actions, and that intertwining good and evil are a part of each postlapsarian [after the Fall] human.

Nevertheless, mankind generally wishes to deny such a frustrating state of being and pretend that it doesn't exist. Steinbeck illustrates this well in Kino and Juana, his protagonists, who reluctantly experience duality. These primitive natives undergo an initiation rite in the novel similar to what

Adam and Eve experienced when they ate from the tree of knowledge of good and evil. This initiation destroys the couple's naïve concept of what man and the world are like and leaves them bereft but wiser in their knowledge of themselves and of their society. Their discovery dispels the illusions of the "good" that surrounds them but also frustrates them as they struggle to cope with a reality which almost always involves a paradoxical yoking of opposites.

Imagery Evokes a Sense of Ambiguity

The yoking of opposites is most obvious in Steinbeck's use of imagery in the novel to portray an intersecting dichotomy of good versus evil. In the novel, sights and sounds as well as symbols are used to compose a pattern of images that offer evidence of the morally ambiguous state that Kino and Juana must contend with.

The first major image Steinbeck uses is a traditional one: light versus darkness. Although several critics have noted that *The Pearl* begins with sunrise and ends in sunset, few have noted that neither the symbolic light nor the lack of it remains the dominant visual image. Instead, light and darkness mingle together to form gray areas where good and evil are inextricably mixed.

Consequently, the reader cannot surmise that the purity and goodness which begin the novel are destroyed and blackened by the sunset which ends the work. In fact, the light/ dark imagery fluctuates between positive and negative connotations just as good and evil do. In addition, the sunrise which begins the day is accompanied by another "positive" image— the harmony of music, the Song of the Family. This sound image also persists in the novel, using another traditional presentation of good's conflict with evil: harmony versus disharmony. Through this image Steinbeck affirms that the beautiful music and its lyric melody, like the early morning, cannot be maintained without the eventual intrusion of discord and dark. . . .

Positive and Negative Are Merged

Steinbeck's use of images becomes syncretic, merging together the various sides of objects and symbols and presenting both the positive and the negative simultaneously. For example, Steinbeck notes that the Song of the Family is quite flexible, and, even though it only has three notes, it possesses an endless variety of intervals. Similarly, although the melody signifies safety, warmth, and wholeness for the couple, it is significant that sometimes the song rises to a sobbing or aching chord that catches in the throat. Ultimately the dual image will expand until the clash of different melodies will indicate Kino's despair at ever being able to achieve harmony in his world.

The merged images of dissonance and darkness continue to preempt the bright music of Juana and are depicted as a threatening song which emanates from a scorpion, Steinbeck's first symbol of the sin and evil which threaten every man. This scorpion and its song conspire against even the innocent tiny baby Coyotito. However, the fact that this scorpion is portrayed as a random evil which invades the couple's lives seems to indicate Steinbeck's belief that the dark side of man's soul is uncontrollable and will eventually attack even the most peaceful, innocent, and harmonious of lives. In short, once again the novel asserts that if a mixture of good and evil is essential to existence, attempts to see only one side of the human condition are futile.

Kino and Juana Discover Evil

However, Juana and Kino, as representatives of an innocent Adam and Eve in the garden, are unaccustomed to the darkness and disharmony that infiltrate human society. Up to this point their lives have been so sheltered that they mistakenly believe that evil exists only in obvious outside forces like the scorpion. Such a force can be smashed into paste by the human hand or foot, and definitely will be overcome in a matter of time. However, once the sting of the evil one touches the baby, his parents begin to discover that their analysis is mistaken and that the evil that the scorpion embodies is impossible to wipe out. Thus, although the physical scorpion is destroyed, it is evident that another springs up in the city of La Paz. Despite the promises of peace that its name suggests, the city provides still further duality as Steinbeck examines the "civilized" community and compares its evil with the scorpion while contrasting it with the goodness of Juana and Kino's primitive existence. As soon as the native couple enter the city seeking help, they begin to learn the lesson that the town does not contain the same warmth and wholeness of their small thatched hut. Moreover, they also note the absence of the moral absolutes that simplified their lives. In the city the evil darkness intermingles intangibly with the good light. It cannot be extracted by folk cures, religion, or ancient spells because it runs rampant among the so-called civilized people, whose avarice and jealousy destroy their potential for good.

Kino and Juana Try to Understand

For example, the doctor who is so essential to the cure of Coyotito is initially associated with the light of education and the blessing of good health. He is seen by the couple as a potential savior, but actually he is the epitome of evil. The ability to distinguish good from evil is thus seen as difficult, at best, and Steinbeck reinforces this dilemma by describing the fine line that separates the two opposites as a "hazy mirage." As Steinbeck describes nature in chapter 2 as poison fish hiding in eel grass and dogs and pigs who feed off the dead, even the positive qualities of the pure surroundings of Juana and Kino are seen as questionable and hiding unknowns. This, of course, parallels a similar uncertainty for Kino and Juana about what is good and what is evil.

Soon the couple will find that nothing is sure and solid, and that moral ambiguity is man's heritage. Yet most critics of

The Pearl have persisted in looking for absolutes and defining the meaning of images within strict boundaries which ultimately did not hold up under close scrutiny. But Steinbeck's parable is not so easily resolved. Chapter 3 begins in brightness as good returns in the form of the great pearl which Kino discovers, the Pearl of the World, gigantic in size and shape. Although not all readers are aware of his literary allusion to the medieval poem also entitled "The Pearl," Steinbeck carefully suggests that even though the gem appears to offer salvation, it is yet another example of the intermixture of good and evil. Specifically, the initial description points out the irony of the pearl's development. It was created because an irritant, a grain of sand, penetrated the oyster's shell and lodged within it. In this incident Steinbeck shows how negatives are at times strangely transformed into positives, and worthless grains of sand become priceless treasures as the oyster works to dispel or neutralize the invading grain, which may cause life-threatening problems.

The Pearl Has Light and Dark Qualities

Once again Steinbeck reintroduces and merges his imagery as the symbolic pearl, which is precious and beyond price, is associated with light. For example, it is "as perfect as the moon. It captured the light and gave it back in silver incandescence. It was as large as a sea-gull's egg. It was the greatest pearl in the world." Yet at the same time the author also uses his light image negatively to stress the moral ambiguity of the gem by stating that the treasure has a ghostly gleam and that Kino mistrusts his perceptions and wonders if the prize might be more illusion than reality.

Elsewhere Steinbeck returns to the music imagery, the Song of the Family, and joins it with the Song of the Pearl That Might Be. At this point the pearl tune is described as a countermelody that blends in with the dominant music, but later in the novel the Song of the Pearl will be associated with something infinitely evil as the narrator notes that "the essence of the pearl was mixed with the essence of men and a curious dark residue was precipitated . . . the schemes, the plans, . . . the lusts, the hungers and . . . he [Kino] became curiously every man's enemy."

Yet Juana and Kino are reluctant to acknowledge the duality they are confronting, for it seems as if their long-sought-for salvation has arrived. Warm and happy in their newfound success and good luck, they can only believe that the music of the family has merged with the music of the pearl so that each beautifies the other.

Kino's Desire for Material Goods

Influenced by this belief, Kino begins to dream of new values and goals, of the light, harmony, and good that the pearl can bring to his life. By seeing only the benefits that the pearl of great price can bring to him, he ignores the treasure's potential for evil, and, unfortunately, his "positive" desires for material goods and for health and education for his son create a negative force in his life. As pride and conceit over his ownership begin to dominate his life, he turns from his former kindly disposition into a man as ruthless and evil as any of the townspeople. A similar irony exists in the fact that although the pearl may solve Kino's problems, Steinbeck reiterates after its discovery that "the dark is almost in". Eventually the coming night becomes a threatening dark that will reveal the greed of Kino's neighbors as they try to steal the pearl from him, turning his dreams into nightmares.

The symbolic pearl is combined with the sight and sound images here as the music of evil suddenly returns to Kino's ears, signifying the duality of the townspeople and the church but also the duality of the gem itself. This music image is described as shrill, as opposed to the sweet music Kino formerly heard from the pearl. Kino, once so positive about his find, now wonders whether anyone or anything can be trusted; his

Michael J. Meyer argues that in The Pearl, *the scorpion that stings the innocent baby Coyotito symbolizes the random and uncontrollable nature of evil.* © CarverMostardi / Alamy.

simple naïvete is being systematically destroyed. Even the medicine prescribed by the doctor is questionable, as Kino cannot help but wonder whether the prescription itself is not evil masquerading as good and whether Coyotito's illness has been caused by the doctor in order to gain the pearl for himself. Such duplicity continues in the narration when the doctor arrives and denies having heard of Kino's good fortune, thus craftily causing Kino to betray the secret hiding place of the treasure.

Conjoined Symbols

The symbols of the scorpion and the pearl, once quite separate and opposite, are now strangely joined, and just as the neighbors were previously associated with the characteristics of the scorpion, so Kino is associated with the pearl. He is no longer pure, but like the oyster is infected by the sands of mistrust and fear. Steinbeck describes the hardness growing over him, but what results for Kino is no treasure. This hardness suggests not wealth but man's animal-like state, where faith and hope in goodness and light and harmony have disappeared as human traits. Soon Kino dreams of darkness, not only a darkness which blots out his own dreams for success but one that also denies the potential of Coyotito's future. Combining this depressing action with sound, Kino begins to recognize that every sound in the world is now an indicator of a dark thing. Kino is transformed into a raging beast, and suddenly the evil side of a primitive life-style is exposed. The formerly docile Kino, his very life now threatened, transforms into a wild animal whose one law is the dark violence of the jungle. Kino has grown in hatred, sin, and wrongdoing, and Steinbeck again suggests that he is similar to the evil part of the pearl: hard, cold, and unyielding.

Despite the use of the negative parallel, Kino still does not understand the concept of the duality of all things. The pearl is still seen as positive because it will provide for a good, the healing of the baby. Yet shortly thereafter, Steinbeck removes this motive as the poison appears to recede from Coyotito's body and it is no longer necessary to use the pearl to obtain the needed payment for the doctor's services. Now the dominant song of joy and happiness is drowned out by Kino's manic desire to keep the pearl at any price, even murder. His readiness to kill in order to keep the treasure leads to the first verbal recognition and admission of the gem's duality. Again an ironic twist is used as Juana, unlike her biblical counterpart Eve, is the first to see the dark elements in the pearl. . . .

After Coyotito's death, Juana and Kino seem removed from the present, and they are transformed into archetypes. The narrator, however, emphasizes the positive rather than the negative side of the experience: "They had gone through pain and had come out on the other side; that there was almost a magical protection about them." Kino now has a new and more accurate vision of the pearl. "He looked into its surface and it was gray and ulcerous. Evil faces peered from it into his eyes, and he saw the light of burning. And in the surface he saw the frantic eyes of the man lying in the pool. And in the surface of the pearl he saw Coyotito lying in the little cave with the top of his head shot away. And the pearl was ugly; it was gray, like a malignant growth. And Kino heard the music of the pearl, distorted and insane."

With this knowledge the relationship of Juana and Kino is restored; both now possess a complete awareness of the pearl's double nature.

Juana Is the Unsung Hero of *The Pearl*

Debra K.S. Barker

Debra K.S. Barker is an associate professor of English and American Indian Studies at the University of Wisconsin–Eau Claire. She is an enrolled member of the Rosebud Sioux Nation (Sicangu Lakota Nation) and has published in the area of American Indian literature and the literature of other people of color.

As the story of The Pearl *begins, Juana is a submissive, obedient character who appears to be dominated by Kino. However, as Barker asserts in the following essay, she undergoes a transformation from innocence and emerges a more powerful individual. Barker suggests that Juana is often overlooked as a heroine in the archetypal role of sage. Juana taps into her own spirituality to sense danger to her family and uses that strength to stand up to authority figures and to Kino. Kino acknowledges Juana's wisdom when he offers her the opportunity to toss the pearl back into the sea. By the end of the story, Kino and Juana walk side by side into the town, a statement of her newfound equality.*

Hurled from the spiritual stasis of innocence into the travail of experience, Juana survives the ultimate initiation experience, transforming into a new being, a powerful character whose role is far more significant than readers have previously recognized. Two particularly important tableaus, when juxtaposed, reveal not only a qualitative change in the dynamics of Kino and Juana's relationship, but also the extent to which Juana's character has grown.

With the first tableau Steinbeck draws of Juana and Kino's relationship, Juana appears as a submissive figure trailing after her husband with a devotion nearly dog-like. Indeed, the narrator's choice of verbs suggests a subordinate status that is less than human. When they venture into La Paz to meet with the pearl dealers, for instance, Juana follows Kino, "trotting after him," later, after he beats her, the narrator describes her as "creeping" along the beach after him. Then as they flee La Paz, we are told that her feet "pad" behind him.

Juana Becomes Kino's Equal

In the second tableau, Juana's elevation to a status equal to Kino's is twice signalled in the final scene in the story, where the narrator mentions that as the two return to La Paz with their murdered infant, they "were not walking in single file, Kino ahead and Juana behind, as usual, but side by side". In this emotionally charged scene, the narrator also reveals not only that Juana seems "removed from human experience," but that her ordeal has scarred and aged both her face and her spirit: "Her face was hard and lined and leathery with fatigue . . . ".

This final scene stands as one of the story's most potent in terms of psychic weight, resonant with the soul-ache of profound bereavement. The scene, with its focus upon both Juana's stoicism and the equal footing with which the two return to their community, prompts us to consider that although Kino is represented as the protagonist and nominal hero of the story, Juana nevertheless undergoes a trial equal to or perhaps more momentous than his. . . .

In the course of the narrative conflict Juana evolves from the role of "Helpmate" to that of "The Sage," a figure elevated to the status of hero because she possesses "wisdom beyond that of the culture." The culture, however, restricts her to "passive heroine roles," even though she "understands the world" and may be fully capable of contending with strife. Such is certainly the case in Juana's circumscribed world, which is not only a colonized one but patriarchal as well.

Juana's Spiritual Vision

Within the role she sustains with Kino, that of wife and help-mate, Juana nevertheless seizes numerous opportunities to assert her powerful will, spiritual vision, and enduring capacity to transcend her own ego to place the needs of her family first. All these traits distinguish her as not only a Hero-Sage, but as one who has syncretized her tribal culture with a modern, Christian one. Ironically, she is yet unaware of her power, deferring to Kino's position as her husband and later to the authority of the white doctor whose medicine she has been taught to believe is more potent than her own. It is Juana, for instance, who reacts quickly to suck the scorpion's poison from Coyotito's shoulder, then invoke the aid of the Christian God, as well as her older ones, with prayers and ceremonies. When they go out to dive for pearls, Juana makes "the magic of prayer, her face set rigid and her muscles hard to force the luck, to tear the luck out of the gods' hands". The narrator notes the irony in the success of Juana's prayer: "She had not prayed directly for the recovery of the baby—she had prayed that they might find a pearl with which to hire the doctor to cure the baby . . .".

As she witnesses Kino's moral deterioration, growing more alarmed as his obsession with the pearl threatens to consume him, she finally begs him to renounce the jewel: "It will destroy us all," Juana prophesies. "Even our son". With Kino's rejection of her entreaties, she performs another ceremony, lighting a candle and crooning the old songs, seeking to bring the sacred into ascendancy within the realm of the secular to foil the evil forces of man and nature operating upon the ordinary world of existence.

As Hero-Sage, Juana possesses a spiritual identification with the natural world that affords her a special insight into its power. She does not have to be told about the trees in the desert that blind and bleed, bringing bad luck. Likewise, she soon recognizes the ineffable power exerted by the pearl, a jewel of the sea which archetypally suggests the emotional depths of the unconscious. When the venom of greed poisons the natures of those from whom they have sought help, she instinctively questions the real value of the pearl in relation to all they must sacrifice for it. Juana says, "Perhaps the dealers were right and the pearl has no value. Perhaps this has all been an illusion". . . .

Kino Recognizes Juana's Wisdom

In its profane aspect, the pearl of Steinbeck's tale evokes the latent materialism of Kino's character, while also stirring the potent forces of the greed and violence within the natures of those obsessed with wrenching the treasure from Kino's grasp. First singing the song of hope, promise, and security for Kino and Juana's future, the pearl comes to sibilate the music of evil and untold suffering. By the end of the story Kino finally recognizes "the music of the pearl" as "distorted" and "insane". As [critic Sydney J.] Krause points out, Kino's own moment of recognition of Juana's prescience is dramatized by his first offering to her the chance to cast the pearl back into the Gulf.

[Literary critics Carol] Pearson and [Katherine] Pope observe that in the case of the Hero-Sage, the female hero often goes unrecognized by the primary male figure in her life who "epitomizes the blindness of the patriarchy to female wisdom and strength". The narrator of *The Pearl* acknowledges both Kino's blindness and Juana's strength: "Sometimes the quality of woman, the reason, the caution, the sense of preservation, could cut through Kino's manness and save them all". Throughout the story, Kino ignores Juana's insistence that the pearl is the source of the evil that threatens their lives; and no more powerfully is Kino's blindness illustrated than when he beats and kicks her after coming upon her as she attempts to throw the pearl into the sea. Echoing [literary critic and Steinbeck scholar] Tetsumaro Hayashi's observation of Juana's instinctive wisdom in allowing Kino's plan to run its course to its tragic conclusion, Pearson and Pope note that the Sage-Hero is keenly aware of "the spiritual dimension of life" since she "ministers to the family's physical needs" and is "more keenly aware of transience and death than a man may be". . . .

Juana's Initiation in the Cave

The initiation of Juana takes place in a mountain cave where she and Coyotito hide while Kino attempts to ambush the trackers. Holding her child, the narrator tells us, "Juana whispered her combination of prayer and magic, her Hail Marys and her ancient intercession, against the black unhuman things". Caves and mountains are traditionally feminine, archetypal symbols of passage. More importantly, mountains, as topographical regions of ascension, suggest points of epiphany, according to [literary critic] Northrop Frye. It is here where "the cyclical world of nature" and the "apocalyptic" realm meet. . . .

In the last stage of the journey, the return, Juana and Kino go back to their village, profoundly bereft not only of the thing they loved most, their child, but also of their innocence and their dreams. . . .

Juana's Spiritual Transformation

Juana's "heroic identities" are realized with a spiritual transformation that brings her to a kind of apotheosis and a transcendence that affords her a point of view from which she has apprehended eternal truths that lie beyond the temporal field of human experience. The narrator speculates that it is as if she had "gone through pain and had come out on the other side"; he observes that Juana's "wide eyes stared inward on herself. She was as remote and as removed as Heaven". With the paradox of the inwardness that is as remote as Heaven, the narrator expresses the numinous quality of Juana's awakening of consciousness. She looks inward because she knows that the source of evil lies not in pearls but, rather, in the human heart.

With the simile "as Heaven," Steinbeck suggests apotheosis and Juana's ascension to a higher, more, divine order of consciousness. . . . For Juana the crisis of the pearl and the death of her son help transform her into an acknowledged equal partner in her marriage as she evolves from Helpmate to Hero. Thus, the concluding tableau of the story points to Juana's recognition of her rebirth as she takes her place alongside Kino when they re-enter the village. Clearly, the profound nature of her suffering has elevated her in both spiritual and secular respects.

The Pearl Bestows the Riches of Mutual Respect

Edward E. Waldron

Edward E. Waldron is a continuing instructor in the Department of English at the University of South Florida. He earned a PhD from Arizona State University. His specialties include American literature and African American literature.

The lead characters in The Pearl *and* The Old Man and the Sea *seek goals beyond the normal expectations of their simple existence. While both protagonists fail to achieve the material rewards they aspire to, states Waldron in the following viewpoint, they gain a renewed sense of dignity. Waldron takes issue with those who interpret the end of* The Pearl *as weak in that it seems Kino is returning to his old life. Instead, he views the conclusion more positively, in that Kino and Juana gain mutual respect.*

There are ... important similarities in the two novels [Ernest Hemingway's *The Old Man and the Sea* (*OMAS*) and John Steinbeck's *The Pearl*]. Both of them, though set in the modern world, center on relatively primitive people. Santiago [the main character in *The Old Man and the Sea*], to be sure, is much more aware of the modern world, especially through his beloved baseball, than are Kino and the people of his village. Still, Santiago fishes as his people always have (he carries no radio, as do some of the other fishermen); and Kino is clearly tied to the ways of his ancestors, in his simple lifestyle and in his recollections of the old songs. Both novels are set in locations that tie men to the sea, and these locations

Edward E. Waldron, "*The Pearl* and *The Old Man and the Sea*: A Comparative Analysis," *Steinbeck Quarterly*, Ball State University, vol. 13, nos. 3 and 4, Summer–Fall 1980, pp. 99, 103–106. Copyright © 1980 by American Journal of Business. All rights reserved. Reproduced by permission.

immediately suggest archetypal patterns of the fight for survival. Although Kino's struggles occur on land, the estuary near his hut offers continual evidence that the natural world is a world of the hunter and the hunted. For all the implied criticism of the social and economic oppression of the Gulf Indians in *The Pearl*, neither novel deals with the modern themes of man against machine or man's alienation in a hostile universe. . . . Instead, the novels focus on the beautiful spectacle of man setting himself a goal and doing his utmost to achieve it, even though he fails in the realization of the material rewards he anticipates. What [literary critic Philip] Young says about Santiago can also be said of Kino and Juana: " . . . his loss has dignity, itself the victory." These protagonists achieve a stature that is worth all the marlins and pearls in the ocean. . . .

Beyond Their Normal Boundaries

Even in the area of thematic concerns, these two novels reflect similar concepts, although there are also obvious differences. In *OMAS* Santiago operates alone in his struggle against the natural forces of the sea. In *The Pearl* Kino and Juana, although separated at one point in their ideas about the pearl, basically function as a pair, a family. In effect, though, the trials of Santiago and the Indian couple come about for the same reason: they "go out too far," the old man to catch his fish and Kino and Juana to seek a fair price for their pearl. And, just as Santiago must fight the sharks to protect his fish, a hopeless endeavor, Kino and Juana must fight the human sharks—the doctor, the "dark ones," the social system itself—to protect their pearl and their lives. . . .

While Steinbeck's ending for *The Pearl* is more ambivalent than Hemingway's ending for *OMAS*, there is a sense of triumph, horribly muted by the death of Coyotito, in the strength that brings Kino and Juana back to their village and allows them to throw the pearl back into the sea. [Literary critic]

Warren French finds the ending terribly weak, mainly because of the "unresolved problems that have been raised by the action" in the novel. "The conclusion of the novel," he continues, "leaves the impression that Kino is returning to his old life. . . . " But are we to conclude that? Is the Kino at the end of the novel the same Kino who began it? And what of his relationship with Juana? If we read this novel as a positive work and not as a study in the inevitable defeat of the common man by the pressures of society, then clearly we must focus on the change that occurs in the characters of Kino and Juana. Examining those changes through the metaphor of the pearl gives us another view of what the *real* "pearl of the world" might be.

> Early in the novel Steinbeck tells us how a pearl is formed:
> An accident could happen to these oysters, a grain of sand could lie in the folds of muscle and irritate the flesh until in self-protection the flesh coated the grain with a layer of smooth cement. But once started, the flesh continued to coat the foreign body until it fell free in some tidal flurry or until the oyster was destroyed.

Kino's timely (and melodramatic) discovery of the great pearl after Coyotito is stung by the scorpion can be read as the accident, the "grain of sand," that starts the process. Until that day, Kino had lived his life as his people had always done; the pattern was as predictable as the tides around which their lives were set. The pearl, however, creates visions for Kino, plans that go against the wishes of the gods. But Kino does not draw back from the attack he knows will come:

> . . . to meet the attack, Kino was already making a hard skin for himself against the world. His eyes and his mind probed for danger before it appeared.

The process has begun.

Immediately, the first irritant appears as the doctor who was too busy to receive Kino earlier in the day comes out to

Actor Spencer Tracy in The Old Man and the Sea *(1958), based on the novel by Ernest Hemingway. Edward E. Waldron draws parallels between* The Pearl *and Hemingway's novel.* © John Springer Collection / Corbis.

his hut to see Coyotito. Trapped by his ignorance, Kino must let the doctor work his "magic" on the baby; but when Coyotito gets worse, Kino remembers the white powder, and "his mind was hard and suspicious . . . ". At least in terms of modern American readers, Kino is becoming a more valuable person as he fights to free himself of the twin tyrannies of ignorance and oppression.

Kino and Juana Gain Mutual Respect

Kino is not alone in this transformation. Juana, a good wife and mother, is a strong woman. While she hears Kino's magnificent visions with awe, she nonetheless is ready to defy him and fling the pearl back to the sea when they are attacked and it becomes clear that the pearl represents a threat to her family. After the struggle that leaves one man dead and Kino beaten, it is Juana who finds the pearl by the path. Realizing "that the old life was gone forever," she strengthens Kino's will once more so they may fly from the danger around them. Leaving the village, Juana pads behind Kino. Returning from their ordeal in the wilderness with the lifeless Coyotito slung in her shawl, however, she walks by Kino's side: " . . . they were not walking in single file, Kino ahead and Juana behind as usual, but side by side . . . and they seemed to carry two towers of darkness with them".

The vision of their return recalled by the villagers is one of mystery:

> The people say that the two seemed to be removed from human experience; that they had gone through pain and had come out on the other side; that there was almost a magical protection about them.

The change is also made clear in their actions regarding the pearl. Acknowledging Juana's strength and courage, Kino offers to let her throw the pearl back; she, in turn acknowledging his strength and courage, insists that he throw it. "*They* [my italics] saw the little splash in the distance, and *they* stood side by side watching the place for a long time". Kino and Juana have lost their child, their hut, and their boat, but they have gained something more valuable, a "pearl beyond price," in their new-found relationship of mutual respect. This change may be more important, again, to middle-class American readers than to the Gulf Indians about whom the tale is told, but its impact remains.

In these two short novels, then, Steinbeck and Hemingway present portraits of triumph in the face of overwhelming adversity, perhaps the most basic of American themes.

Kino's Dreams for the Pearl Transcend Personal Greed

S.S. Prabhakar Rao

S.S. Prabhakar Rao is on the faculty of ICFAI University, Hyderabad, India, where he was formerly professor of English. A distinguished translator of the Telugu language of India, he has published five anthologies of poetry translated from Telugu. The Golden Bouquet, a collection of writings by Rao, includes critical reviews of works by Steinbeck, as well as by George Orwell, Chinua Achebe, and Saul Bellow.

In the following selection, Rao asserts that Steinbeck changed the original parable of the pearl to make it more universally satisfying and substantive. Instead of a young single man with limited vision, Kino is portrayed as seeking something much more important than women and drinking. Instead of rewards that benefit only his own ego, Kino dreams of how the pearl will benefit his family. The goals he seeks are those that will free the family from oppression. The first is freedom to practice their religion in a church, which has been denied them because of their poverty. Second, Kino wants to buy a rifle to protect his family from those who would exploit them. Third, Kino dreams of an education for his son, so he can shake off the restraints of poverty. After Coyotito's death, however, the pearl is of no value to Kino.

The Dream of Kino in *The Pearl* would appear to reveal a reversal in the social attitude of Steinbeck. Both in *Tortilla Flat* and *Cannery Row* Steinbeck pilloried middle-class respectability. His views on what society considers as 'success' have been well-known and have also integrated into the two

S.S. Prabhakar Rao, "The Dream and the Shadow," *John Steinbeck: A Study (Motifs of Dream and Disillusionment)*, Hyderabad, India: Academic Publishers, 1976, pp. 160–163.

novels. One might dispute their social relevance in the novels. But here Steinbeck seems to portray in Kino a dream of attaining just this kind of 'success' which money could ensure for him.

However, a careful study of the novelette would reveal that the reversal of attitude is more apparent than real. After *The Grapes of Wrath*, it is in this novel that Steinbeck seems to re-create authentically both the locale of action and the dream of his protagonist. A comparison of the fable he told in the novelette with the story he heard during his expedition to the Sea of Cortez, in [La] Paz, would show how Steinbeck made out of a crude character a more satisfyingly universal symbol of man's aspiration to get out of his station in life and of the inevitable defeat in such an enterprise. The ambition of the fisherman in the original story was merely 'to be drunk as long as he wished, to marry any one of a number of girls and to make many more a little happy too.'

The dream of Kino extends beyond mere carousing. His dream of the money, which he would make by selling the greatest pearl in the world he finds in the sea, is not related to any egoistic pleasure of his own. He wants the pearl rather for the sake of the family. In fact, the dream extends even further; it assumes a racial significance, inasmuch as he seeks it to liberate his race from its accustomed surrender to the whiteman's repression largely on account of the lack of education.

Kino Wants the Pearl to Benefit His People

At first, the dream of finding a pearl arises out of a need for personal revenge against the doctor who refused to treat his son stung by the scorpion, because he could not pay him. When he does find the great pearl, his vague dream takes on concrete dimensions. The dream now takes a three-fold significance for Kino and the men of his race. It is in this portrayal of a dream beyond the narrow personal need that the tale acquires archetypal references. The dream, first, is for religion denied to them on account of their poverty. He tells his brother, Juan Tomas: 'We will be married—in the church,' because now they could buy religion.

The second aspect of the dream relates to a rifle, a symbol of protection from the predatory onslaughts of the Spaniard, who is later in the story symbolized by the man on horseback, Kino's pursuer in his ill-fated flight from the town. In his vision of the future, 'Kino saw Kino in the pearl, Kino holding a Winchester Carbine.' The need for a rifle also is a need beyond personal safety; it is a need of a whole race of people. The third aspect of the dream is an aspiration for education for Kino's son, Coyotito. Kino goes into a rhapsodic prophecy over this:

> 'My son', he exclaims, 'will read and open books and my son will make numbers, and these things will make us free because he will know; he will know and through him we will know.'

Thus the dream of Kino, in its three-fold dimension, transcends narrow egoism; it is symbolic of the dream of his race. Steinbeck seems in this novelette to have matched his intention with performance, as, in following the story of Kino, we do tend 'to look beyond the physical events to their spiritual significance.'

In his determined pursuit of the dream, Kino is determined that his son must liberate his race through the force of education. When his brother advises him to get rid of the pearl, which appears to cause more harm than good, he remonstrates: 'This is our chance. Our son must go to school. He must break out of the pot that holds us in.'

Kino Defies the System

The adversary against whom Kino pits himself is indeed formidable. Again, as elsewhere, Steinbeck does not locate the villain in any single individual, but in an unsympathetic social and economic arrangement, devised to exploit the weaker sections of the society for the profit of the manoeuvring minority. Here the pearl-buyers are not villains by themselves, but part of the system which keeps the individual down at his station in society. There is only one pearl-buyer with several agents to keep the price of the pearls low: 'there was only one pearl-buyer with several hands.'

Kino, however, seeks to defy the whole system and to get out of his station. It is this defiance which appears to Juan Tomas as his principal indiscretion. He tells Kino: 'you have defied not the pearl-buyers, but the whole structure, the whole way of life.' But it is important to note that neither Juan Tomas nor the earlier Steinbeck would find fault with Kino for his defiance. Juan, for instance, is aware that they 'are cheated from birth to the overcharge on our coffins.' For the early Steinbeck a courageous defiance of an inimical order, even in the face of certain defeat, is an admirable characteristic of man. By and large, Kino is one of Steinbeck's 'positive' men inasmuch as he does not give up his resistance easily. Even when the hired men of the buyers raid his house and beat him up, despite his wife's appeal 'to destroy the pearl before it destroys us,' he declares, almost like [Captain] Ahab [in Herman Melville's *Moby Dick*]: 'I will fight this thing. I will win over it. We will have our chance ... Believe me, I am a man.'

Kino's Dream Shattered by Coyotito's Death

Towards the end, the nerve of Kino is hopelessly shattered not on account of what happens to him personally but on account of the destruction of the fulcrum of his grand aspirations, when his son is shot by one of his faceless pursuers. As the dream of liberation from the subjugation of his race through the education of his son is ruined, the pearl becomes to him a thing of no value.

The cathedral in La Paz, Mexico, where The Pearl *is set. S.S. Prabhakar Rao argues that Kino's dreams for the pearl are not for himself but for his family; he wants freedom from oppression, a church wedding for Juana, and an education for Coyotito.* © John Mitchell / Alamy.

At first, the pearl raises in him great hopes—the three-fold dream already discussed. It has almost become his soul. He tells his brother, who advises him to throw away the pearl:

> the pearl has become my soul. If I give it up, I shall lose my soul.

But towards the end, the pearl appears to him as the source of all evil. As he studies the pearl before flinging it into the sea, he sees that 'evil faces peered from it into his eyes, and he saw the light of burning . . . And the pearl was ugly; it was grey like a malignant growth.' It is the killing of his son which shatters his faith in the pearl. They return to their village, purged of their illusions concerning the efficacy of the pearl. Further, as pointed out earlier, the pearl has never been a source of desire for personal enrichment, which is why, in-stead of proceeding to the town [to] sell it for a higher amount and live on happily . . . , they return to their earlier life of routine obedience. With the death of his son, the dream has lost for him both its relevance and significance.

A Tragic Triumph

The final act of Kino is consciously symbolic, but its symbolism is imprecise and lends itself to a variety of interpretations. As Steinbeck wrote in the introductory note to the fable, 'perhaps everyone takes his own meaning from it and reads his own life into it.' Apparently, Kino is defeated by the inhuman forces of commerce in his attempts to defy the whole system. He has thrown himself against the rocks and is beaten completely. And yet in his defeat it is possible to find a certain assertion—an element of tragic triumph—of his individuality too. By throwing away the pearl rather than let himself be cheated by the system, he does act independently.

The Pearl Inspires Kino to Fight the Poverty and Degradation of His People

Kyoko Ariki

Kyoko Ariki is a professor of English at Okayama College, a private women's college in Japan. Ariki has published articles and books on Steinbeck and coedited Re-reading John Steinbeck.

Kino believes that escaping poverty and overcoming ignorance are the keys to freedom and self-esteem. In Ariki's view in the following selection, Kino becomes aware of the social injustices visited on his people by people such as the doctor and the pearl buyers. After Kino loses the things most precious to him—including his son—he cannot return to his innocent state. Ariki concludes that Steinbeck leaves the end of the story open to the reader's interpretation and expects that Kino will educate his people about their exploitation and lead them to fight for dignity.

Pepe in [Steinbeck's short story] "Flight" and Kino in *The Pearl* are Native Americans who ranked at the bottom of society, were extremely poor, and were obliged to lead an almost subhuman life. . . .

In *The Pearl* Kino, who . . . lives in a shabby brush house, leads a very simple and poor life with his wife Juana and his baby son, Coyotito. At the beginning Kino is contented with his peaceful life; he even "sighs with satisfaction". But an accident makes him aware of the humiliating situations he and his people have been forced to endure. When their baby is stung by a scorpion, Kino and Juana take him to the doctor,

Kyoko Ariki, "From 'Flight' to *The Pearl*: A Thematic Study," *Steinbeck Review*, vol. 3, no. 1, Spring 2006, pp. 86–88, 90–92, 94.

but the physician is greedy and not interested in poor people, ordering his servant to tell them that he is not at home. Kino sees through his lies and feels humiliated:

> For a long time Kino stood in front of the gate with Juana beside him. Slowly he put his suppliant hat on his head. Then, without warning, he struck the gate a crushing blow with his fist. He looked down in wonder at his split knuckles and at the blood that flowed down between his fingers.

Kino's Realization

Rejected by this insolent doctor, Kino finds his humiliation turning to fury. If his son had not been [stung] by a scorpion or if he had not found the pearl of the world, he might have remained contented with his peaceful life. The discovery of the pearl makes him realize how unfairly his people have been exploited by the doctor and people like him. Steinbeck writes, "This doctor was of a race which for nearly four hundred years had beaten and starved and robbed and despised Kino's race, and frightened it too, so that the indigene came humbly to the door". It is obvious that not only the doctor but the pearl buyers who try to cheat Kino belong to the same race. In *The Pearl* the social status of the Indians is described in more detail than in "Flight." While Kino and his people lead poor lives in shabby brush huts near the beach, the doctor, whose "race" defeated Kino's many years ago, lives in a fancy house which symbolizes his social status. His house has "harsh outer walls and inner cool gardens where a little water played and the bougainvillea [crusted] the walls with purple and brick-red and white".

The Pearl Is a Path to Dignity and Pride

When Kino finds the pearl of the world, he sees in it the possibility of escaping poverty and persecution. He dreams of having a marriage ceremony with Juana at a church, of buying a rifle, and of sending his son to school. His dreams are all associated with his respectability and dignity as a human being. He thinks a rifle and education are powerful weapons for breaking out of the cage in which his people are shut. Sensing the devilish nature of the pearl, however, Juana pleads with her husband to throw it away—a plea that Kino does not heed. He believes that the pearl will be the only chance to become rich enough to get what he wants and restore his pride. For Kino, getting out of poverty and overcoming ignorance are short cuts to the freedom and self-esteem essential for human beings. He says, "Our son must go to school. He must break out of the pot that holds us in". That is why he hangs on to the pearl and kills the men who try to rob him of it. . . .

Kino Becomes Outraged by Injustice

In *The Pearl* the historical background of the Indians and their status in society is depicted more definitely and in more detail [than in "Flight"]. Unlike the main figure in "Flight," the protagonist of *The Pearl* has a family—making the story both richer and darker. When Kino accidentally kills a man in a fight while trying to protect himself, he decides he must leave his town, knowing full well what will happen to an Indian who kills someone, whether in self-defense or not. Although Kino is like Pepé because he has to leave his home after killing a man, his flight does not necessarily suggest a journey to death. . . . Kino has attempted to escape the humiliating situation in which his people have been imprisoned for such a long time. While Pepé is not concerned about social injustice, Kino becomes aware of it and becomes angry when he is insulted or cheated by the doctor or the pearl buyers. When Kino discovers that the pearl buyers have tried to cheat him, he cries, "Some deep outrage is here. My son must have a chance". Because the canoe is his family's pride and one of his precious few possessions, he is infuriated when he sees a great hole at the bottom of his canoe, and "a searing rage came to him and gave him strength" . . .

View of a cove at La Paz, Baja California Sur. The Pearl *is based on a story Steinbeck heard when he visited La Paz in 1941.* © Reinhard Dirscherl / Alamy.

Awareness Prevents Return to Ignorance

Kino loses everything—his house, his canoe, and his son. When he returns to their hometown with Juana and his dead son, he throws the pearl back into the ocean. He still has the rifle and his wife, Juana—a highly symbolic ending. Though [literary critic] Warren French argues that "the conclusion of the novel leaves the impression that Kino is returning to his old life," the renunciation of the pearl does not simply mean that Kino and his wife will go back to their original life. It is not possible for him to do so, because he has killed four people who apparently belong to a higher class. He will probably be arrested and executed. Further, because he has broken community rules, the people in his town will no longer accept him.

Kino's brother Juan Tomas says to him, "We do know we are cheated from birth to the overcharge on our coffins. But we survive. You have defied not the pearl buyers, but the whole structure, the whole way of life, and I am afraid for you". But there is another reason—probably an insurmountable one—that prevents Kino from regaining his original life. Once Kino has learned about the unfair structure of his society, he cannot return to his former state of contented ignorance. The only path for him is to stand up and fight. In doing so, he needs to enlighten his people. . . . For if Kino stands up for his beliefs, leads an awakened people, and fights . . . he may succeed in regaining his people's pride. . . . This finale is what the reader expects of Kino at the story's end. And this is what Steinbeck wants readers to do—to create Kino's future story. . . .

Motivated to Stand Up for His People

The Pearl ends in tragedy, but, unlike "Flight," it leaves hope—a hope that Kino will stand up to change the social system by fighting together with his people. Kino demonstrates his strong determination to regain freedom and a respectable life without depending on the pearl when he throws it into the ocean. Kino is an awakened Pepé. . . .

In "Flight" Steinbeck depicts the wretched conditions in which the Mexican Indians live, implying that there is no other way for Pepé to achieve manhood but to die courageously. In *The Pearl*, however, Kino refuses to be killed, humiliated and exploited. At first glance indeed *The Pearl* is based on the story Steinbeck heard when he visited La Paz during an expedition to the Mexican Gulf, but the role of the pearl differs in the two stories. The pearl Kino finds serves as a catalyst which awakens him and changes him, while the pearl in the original story is simply a means to fortune or wealth. For not until Kino finds the pearl does he realize that his life is humiliating. Both protagonists lose precious possessions one after another, but Kino does not lose everything— Juana is still with him.

The reader knows that as long as Juana is there, Kino will never yield to circumstances but will stand up to fight for their future.

Social Issues
in Literature

CHAPTER 3

Contemporary
Perspectives on Poverty

The "Culture of Poverty" Perpetuates Distorted Views of the Poor

Paul Gorski

Paul Gorski is assistant professor of integrative studies, with a specialty in social justice education, at George Mason University in Virginia. He is also the founder of EdChange, a coalition dedicated to achieving educational equity in schools and communities.

According to Gorski in the following article, the theory of the culture of poverty is a myth, as has been proven by recent studies. Gorski says the underlying assumptions of the premise are based on classism, which assumes poor people are somehow deficient. The deficit theory can be used to justify giving privileges to economically advantaged students, without equal treatment for poor students. Gorski cites classism in examples such as lower funding for schools that serve poor students, substandard facilities, and larger class sizes. This opportunity gap can be corrected only when the underlying beliefs of classism are addressed.

As the students file out of Janet's classroom, I sit in the back corner, scribbling a few final notes. Defeat in her eyes, Janet drops into a seat next to me with a sigh.

"I *love* these kids," she declares, as if trying to convince me. "I adore them. But my hope is fading."

"Why's that?" I ask, stuffing my notes into a folder.

"They're smart. I know they're smart, but ... "

And then the deficit floodgates open. "They don't care about school. They're unmotivated. And their parents—I'm

Paul Gorski, "The Myth of the 'Culture of Poverty,'" *Educational Leadership*, vol. 65, no. 7, April 2008, pp. 32–36. Copyright © 2008 by ASCD. Reprinted and adapted with permission. Learn more about ASCD at www.ascd.org.

lucky if two or three of them show up for conferences. No wonder the kids are unprepared to learn."

At Janet's invitation, I spent dozens of hours in her classroom, meeting her students, observing her teaching, helping her navigate the complexities of an urban midwestern elementary classroom with a growing percentage of students in poverty. I observed powerful moments of teaching and learning, caring and support. And I witnessed moments of internal conflict in Janet, when what she wanted to believe about her students collided with her prejudices.

Like most educators, Janet is determined to create an environment in which each student reaches his or her full potential. And like many of us, despite overflowing with good intentions, Janet has bought into the most common and dangerous myths about poverty.

Chief among these is the "culture of poverty" myth—the idea that poor people share more or less monolithic and predictable beliefs, values, and behaviors. For educators like Janet to be the best teachers they can be for all students, they need to challenge this myth and reach a deeper understanding of class and poverty.

A Culture of Poverty Assumes Shared Cultural Values

Oscar Lewis coined the term *culture of poverty* in his 1961 book *The Children of Sanchez*. Lewis based his thesis on his ethnographic studies of small Mexican communities. His studies uncovered approximately 50 attributes shared within these communities: frequent violence, a lack of a sense of history, a neglect of planning for the future, and so on. Despite studying very small communities, Lewis extrapolated his findings to suggest a universal culture of poverty. More than 45 years later, the premise of the culture of poverty paradigm remains the same: that people in poverty share a consistent and observable "culture."

Lewis ignited a debate about the nature of poverty that continues today. But just as important—especially in the age of data-driven decision making—he inspired a flood of research. Researchers around the world tested the culture of poverty concept empirically. Others analyzed the overall body of evidence regarding the culture of poverty paradigm.

A Culture of Poverty Does Not Exist

These studies raise a variety of questions and come to a variety of conclusions about poverty. But on this they all agree: *There is no such thing as a culture of poverty.* Differences in values and behaviors among poor people are just as great as those between poor and wealthy people.

In actuality, the culture of poverty concept is constructed from a collection of smaller stereotypes which, however false, seem to have crept into mainstream thinking as unquestioned fact. Let's look at some examples.

MYTH: Poor people are unmotivated and have weak work ethics.

The Reality: Poor people do not have weaker work ethics or lower levels of motivation than wealthier people. Although poor people are often stereotyped as lazy, 83 percent of children from low-income families have at least one employed parent; close to 60 percent have at least one parent who works full-time and year-round. In fact, the severe shortage of living-wage jobs means that many poor adults must work two, three, or four jobs. According to the Economic Policy Institute (2002), poor working adults spend more hours working each week than their wealthier counterparts.

MYTH: Poor parents are uninvolved in their children's learning, largely because they do not value education.

The Reality: Low-income parents hold the same attitudes about education that wealthy parents do. Low-income parents are less likely to attend school functions or volunteer in their children's classrooms—not because they care less about educa-

97

tion, but because they have less access to school involvement than their wealthier peers. They are more likely to work multiple jobs, to work evenings, to have jobs without paid leave, and to be unable to afford child care and public transportation. It might be said more accurately that schools that fail to take these considerations into account do not value the involvement of poor families as much as they value the involvement of other families.

MYTH: Poor people are linguistically deficient.

The Reality: All people, regardless of the languages and language varieties they speak, use a full continuum of language registers. What's more, linguists have known for decades that all language varieties are highly structured with complex grammatical rules. What often are assumed to be *deficient* varieties of English—Appalachian varieties, perhaps, or what some refer to as Black English Vernacular—are no less sophisticated than so-called "standard English."

MYTH: Poor people tend to abuse drugs and alcohol.

The Reality: Poor people are no more likely than their wealthier counterparts to abuse alcohol or drugs. Although drug sales are more visible in poor neighborhoods, drug use is equally distributed across poor, middle class, and wealthy communities. [Researchers have] found that alcohol consumption is *significantly higher* among upper-middle-class white high school students than among poor black high school students. Their finding supports a history of research showing that alcohol abuse is far more prevalent among wealthy people than among poor people. In other words, considering alcohol and illicit drugs together, wealthy people are more likely than poor people to be substance abusers.

The Problem Is a Culture of Classism

The myth of a "culture of poverty" distracts us from a dangerous culture that does exist—the culture of classism. This culture continues to harden in our schools today. It leads the most well intentioned of us, like my friend Janet, into low expectations for low-income students. It makes teachers fear their most powerless pupils. And, worst of all, it diverts attention from what people in poverty do have in common: inequitable access to basic human rights.

The most destructive tool of the culture of classism is deficit theory. In education, we often talk about the deficit perspective—defining students by their weaknesses rather than their strengths. Deficit theory takes this attitude a step further, suggesting that poor people are poor because of their own moral and intellectual deficiencies. Deficit theorists use two strategies for propagating this world view: (1) drawing on well-established stereotypes, and (2) ignoring systemic conditions, such as inequitable access to high-quality schooling, that support the cycle of poverty.

The implications of deficit theory reach far beyond individual bias. If we convince ourselves that poverty results not from gross inequities (in which we might be complicit) but from poor people's own deficiencies, we are much less likely to support authentic antipoverty policy and programs. Further, if we believe, however wrongly, that poor people don't value education, then we dodge any responsibility to redress the gross education inequities with which they contend. This application of deficit theory establishes the idea of what [social scientist H.J.] Gans calls the *undeserving poor*—a segment of our society that simply does not deserve a fair shake.

If the goal of deficit theory is to justify a system that privileges economically advantaged students at the expense of working-class and poor students, then it appears to be working marvelously. In our determination to "fix" the mythical culture of poor students, we ignore the ways in which our society cheats them out of opportunities that their wealthier peers take for granted. We ignore the fact that poor people suffer disproportionately the effects of nearly every major social ill. They lack access to health care, living-wage jobs, safe and affordable housing, clean air and water, and so on—conditions that limit their abilities to achieve to their full potential.

Perhaps most of us, as educators, feel powerless to address these bigger issues. But the question is this: Are we willing, at the very least, to tackle the classism in our own schools and classrooms?

Classism in Education Is Well Documented

This classism is plentiful and well documented. For example, compared with their wealthier peers, poor students are more likely to attend schools that have less funding; lower teacher salaries; more limited computer and internet access; larger class sizes; higher student-to-teacher ratios; a less-rigorous curriculum; and fewer experienced teachers. The National Commission on Teaching and America's Future (2004) also found that low-income schools were more likely to suffer from cockroach or rat infestation, dirty or inoperative student bathrooms, large numbers of teacher vacancies and substitute teachers, more teachers who are not licensed in their subject areas, insufficient or outdated classroom materials, and inadequate or nonexistent learning facilities, such as science labs.

Here in Minnesota, several school districts offer universal half-day kindergarten but allow those families that can afford to do so to pay for full-day services. Our poor students scarcely make it out of early childhood without paying the price for our culture of classism. Deficit theory requires us to ignore these inequities—or worse, to see them as normal and justified.

What does this mean? Regardless of how much students in poverty value education, they must overcome tremendous inequities to learn. Perhaps the greatest myth of all is the one that dubs education the "great equalizer." Without considerable change, it cannot be anything of the sort.

There Is a New Approach to Examining the Culture of Poverty

Patricia Cohen

Patricia Cohen is a culture reporter for the New York Times, *where she has covered ideas and intellectual life since 2007. She has also worked at the* Washington Post, Rolling Stone, *and* Newsday.

The term "culture of poverty" was used in the 1960s to describe urban black families who were perceived as living in a self-perpetuated cycle of welfare, unwed motherhood, and poverty. The term was largely discredited as assigning blame to people for causing their own misfortune. However, states Patricia Cohen in the following essay, the concept is being revisited as cultural values change and poverty in the United States is at a fifteen-year high. The new approach takes into account racism, shared community standards, and the structures of neighborhoods. Cohen notes that some sociologists are still concerned about a definition of poverty that blames the victim.

For more than 40 years, social scientists investigating the causes of poverty have tended to treat cultural explanations like [the Harry Potter series villain] Lord Voldemort: That Which Must Not Be Named.

The reticence was a legacy of the ugly battles that erupted after [US senator] Daniel Patrick Moynihan, then an assistant labor secretary in the [President Lyndon] Johnson administration, introduced the idea of a "culture of poverty" to the public in a startling 1965 report. Although Moynihan didn't coin the phrase (that distinction belongs to the anthropologist Oscar Lewis), his description of the urban black family as caught in an inescapable "tangle of pathology" of unmarried mothers and welfare dependency was seen as attributing self-perpetuating moral deficiencies to black people, as if blaming them for their own misfortune.

A Controversial Theory

Moynihan's analysis never lost its appeal to conservative thinkers, whose arguments ultimately succeeded when President Bill Clinton signed a bill in 1996 "ending welfare as we know it." But in the overwhelmingly liberal ranks of academic sociology and anthropology the word "culture" became a live grenade, and the idea that attitudes and behavior patterns kept people poor was shunned.

Now, after decades of silence, these scholars are speaking openly about you-know-what, conceding that culture and persistent poverty are enmeshed.

Academics Are Revisiting the Culture Theory

"We've finally reached the stage where people aren't afraid of being politically incorrect," said Douglas S. Massey, a sociologist at Princeton who has argued that Moynihan was unfairly maligned.

The old debate has shaped the new. Last month [September 2010] Princeton and the Brookings Institution released a collection of papers on unmarried parents, a subject, it noted, that became off-limits after the Moynihan report. At the recent annual meeting of the American Sociological Association, attendees discussed the resurgence of scholarship on culture. And in Washington last spring, social scientists participated in a Congressional briefing on culture and poverty linked to a special issue of *The Annals*, the journal of the American Academy of Political and Social Science.

"Culture is back on the poverty research agenda," the introduction declares, acknowledging that it should never have been removed.

Legislators Are Interested in Poverty Again

The topic has generated interest on Capitol Hill because so much of the research intersects with policy debates. Views of the cultural roots of poverty "play important roles in shaping how lawmakers choose to address poverty issues," Representative Lynn Woolsey, Democrat of California, noted at the briefing.

This surge of academic research also comes as the percentage of Americans living in poverty hit a 15-year high: one in seven, or 44 million.

With these studies come many new and varied definitions of culture, but they all differ from the '60s-era model in these crucial respects: Today, social scientists are rejecting the notion of a monolithic and unchanging culture of poverty. And they attribute destructive attitudes and behavior not to inherent moral character but to sustained racism and isolation.

Newer Theories Attribute Poverty to Community Norms

To Robert J. Sampson, a sociologist at Harvard, culture is best understood as "shared understandings."

"I study inequality, and the dominant focus is on structures of poverty," he said. But he added that the reason a neighborhood turns into a "poverty trap" is also related to a common perception of the way people in a community act and think. When people see graffiti and garbage, do they find it acceptable or see serious disorder? Do they respect the legal system or have a high level of "moral cynicism," believing that "laws were made to be broken"?

As part of a large research project in Chicago, Professor Sampson walked through different neighborhoods this summer, dropping stamped, addressed envelopes to see how many people would pick up an apparently lost letter and mail it, a sign that looking out for others is part of the community's culture.

In some neighborhoods, like Grand Boulevard, where the notorious Robert Taylor public housing projects once stood, almost no envelopes were mailed; in others researchers received more than half of the letters back. Income levels did not necessarily explain the difference, Professor Sampson said, but rather the community's cultural norms, the levels of moral cynicism and disorder.

The shared perception of a neighborhood—is it on the rise or stagnant?—does a better job of predicting a community's future than the actual level of poverty, he said.

William Julius Wilson, whose pioneering work boldly confronted ghetto life while focusing on economic explanations for persistent poverty, defines culture as the way "individuals in a community develop an understanding of how the world works and make decisions based on that understanding."

For some young black men, Professor Wilson, a Harvard sociologist, said, the world works like this: "If you don't develop a tough demeanor, you won't survive. If you have access to weapons, you get them, and if you get into a fight, you have to use them."

Findings Challenge Common Assumptions

Seeking to recapture the topic from economists, sociologists have ventured into poor neighborhoods to delve deeper into the attitudes of residents. Their results have challenged some common assumptions, like the belief that poor mothers remain single because they don't value marriage.

In Philadelphia, for example, low-income mothers told the sociologists Kathryn Edin and Maria Kefalas that they thought marriage was profoundly important, even sacred, but doubted that their partners were "marriage material." Their results have prompted some lawmakers and poverty experts to conclude that programs that promote marriage without changing economic and social conditions are unlikely to work.

Mario Luis Small, a sociologist at the University of Chicago and an editor of *The Annals'* special issue, tried to figure out why some New York City mothers with children in day care developed networks of support while others did not. As he explained in his 2009 book, "Unanticipated Gains," the answer did not depend on income or ethnicity, but rather the rules of the day-care institution. Centers that held frequent field trips, organized parents' associations and had pick-up and drop-off procedures created more opportunities for parents to connect.

Younger academics like Professor Small, 35, attributed the upswing in cultural explanations to a "new generation of scholars without the baggage of that debate."

Scholars like Professor Wilson, 74, who have tilled the field much longer, mentioned the development of more sophisticated data and analytical tools. He said he felt compelled to look more closely at culture after the publication of Charles Murray and Richard Herrnstein's controversial 1994 book, "The Bell Curve," which attributed African-Americans' lower I.Q. scores to genetics.

The authors claimed to have taken family background into account, Professor Wilson said, but "they had not captured the cumulative effects of living in poor, racially segregated neighborhoods."

He added, "I realized we needed a comprehensive measure of the environment, that we must consider structural *and* cultural forces."

He mentioned a study by Professor Sampson, 54, that found that growing up in areas where violence limits socializing outside the family and where parents haven't attended college stunts verbal ability, lowering I.Q. scores by as much as six points, the equivalent of missing more than a year in school.

Changing Social Mores Have Opened the Debate

Changes outside campuses have made conversation about the cultural roots of poverty easier than it was in the '60s. Divorce, living together without marrying, and single motherhood are now commonplace. At the same time prominent African-Americans have begun to speak out on the subject. In 2004 the comedian Bill Cosby made headlines when he criticized poor blacks for "not parenting" and dropping out of school.

President [Barack] Obama, who was abandoned by his father, has repeatedly talked about "responsible fatherhood."

Conservatives also deserve credit, said Kay S. Hymowitz, a fellow at the conservative Manhattan Institute, for their sustained focus on family values and marriage even when cultural explanations were disparaged.

Do Theories Still Blame the Victim?

Still, worries about blaming the victim persist. Policy makers and the public still tend to view poverty through one of two competing lenses, Michèle Lamont, another editor of the special issue of *The Annals*, said: "Are the poor poor because they are lazy, or are the poor poor because they are a victim of the markets?"

So even now some sociologists avoid words like "values" and "morals" or reject the idea that, as *The Annals* put it, "a group's culture is more or less coherent." Watered-down definitions of culture, Ms. Hymowitz complained, reduce some of the new work to "sociological pablum."

"If anthropologists had come away from doing field work in New Guinea concluding 'everyone's different,' but sometimes people help each other out," she wrote in an e-mail, "there would be no field of anthropology—and no word culture for cultural sociologists to bend to their will."

Fuzzy definitions or not, culture is back. This prompted mock surprise from Rep. Woolsey at last spring's Congressional briefing: "What a concept. Values, norms, beliefs play very important roles in the way people meet the challenges of poverty."

The Shooting of a Mexican Teen Magnifies Conflict Along the US-Mexican Border

Daniela Pastrana

Daniela Pastrana reports on Latin American social and political news and issues for the IPS (Inter Press Service) News Agency, a global news agency with a mission of giving a voice to the voiceless. IPS News was founded in 1964.

A US Border Patrol officer fatally shot Mexican teenager Sergio Hernández from the El Paso, Texas, side of the border. The shooting ignited a public outcry on the Juárez, Mexico, side of the border. Prior to tightened border security, people were known to come and go freely from Juárez to El Paso. But, as Pastrana states in the essay that follows, in the post-9/11 world, stricter security has had a negative impact on the relations between the two cities. Juárez is rife with drug-related violence and murders, and its poverty level is increasing rapidly. El Paso, says Pastrana, is the second-safest city in the United States and has enjoyed steady economic growth. Pastrana reports that hostilities toward immigrants are on the rise all along the US-Mexican border.

"Sergio, your death will be avenged by the angry, organised people" reads graffiti under the Puente Negro railroad bridge connecting this border city [Juárez] with El Paso, Texas.

The message was spray-painted by a few dozen youngsters who gathered in this spot on the border on Jun. 12 [2010]. Five days earlier, on Jun. 7, a U.S. border patrol officer had opened fire from the El Paso side of the border on a 15-year-old Mexican boy, Sergio Hernández, who was with a group of boys throwing stones under the bridge across the nearly dry riverbed of the Rio Grande.

The fatal shooting, caught on a cell-phone camera by someone who was walking across the nearby Paso del Norte or Santa Fe bridge, has galvanised public opinion in Juárez, a city devastated by drug-related violence and nearly two decades of unsolved murders of hundreds of poor young women, as well as a severe recession.

Protesters Decry Excessive Force

"There is a huge sense of outrage, not only because he was just a boy, but because of the cruelty and the excessive use of forces," Rodolfo Rubio, a researcher at the Colegio de la Frontera Norte, a college in northern Mexico that specialises in migration issues, told IPS [the Inter Press Service News Agency].

The history of Ciudad Juárez is indelibly marked by its location on the border between Mexico and the U.S. When Texas was annexed in 1845, the original city, El Paso del Norte, was divided by the Rio Grande, known in Mexico as the Rio Bravo, which today has a double chain link fence running along it on the U.S. side.

Three decades ago, at the spot where the graffiti calling for justice for Sergio can be seen, people from Ciudad Juáarez would often cross the river several times a day on inner tubes, to visit their relatives in El Paso.

Studies show that 75 percent of the people of El Paso are Hispanic. Rubio said the border in Juárez-El Paso is more porous than in any other border city.

Post-9/11 Security Is Much Tighter

But relations between the two cities changed "substantially" as a result of the tighter security adopted on the U.S. side after the Sept. 11, 2001 terror attacks on New York and Washington, the expert on migration issues said.

"Relations, both social and commercial, are divided now," he said.

César Fuentes, an expert on binational development, said one of the "first negative impacts" of that policy was the increased time it takes to cross the border, which means people "go to El Paso less frequently and stay longer when they do."

The rampant violence on the Mexican side of the border has also given an unexpected boost to the economy in El Paso. The El Paso Hispanic Chamber of Commerce (EPHCC) reports that more than 200 Mexican companies opened their doors in that city in 2009, a 40 percent increase over the previous year.

"The services sector, especially restaurants, has grown. And so has real estate," Fuentes said.

The contrast between the two sides of the border is stark.

Violence Is Rampant in Juárez

As many as 800 women in Juárez, many of them workers from the maquila export assembly plants, have been raped, tortured and murdered since 1993. And the wave of violence triggered by the federal government's all-out offensive against drug trafficking cartels has left 5,400 people dead in the last three years.

Meanwhile, El Paso, a city of 700,000, is ranked as the second safest large city in the U.S. after Honolulu, the capital of Hawaii.

In the first six months of this year [2010], more than 1,800 people were murdered in Juárez, compared to just one in El Paso.

The already high poverty level in Ciudad Juárez, which has a population of 1.7 million, is growing fast as the maquila plants, which pay low wages and import materials and equipment duty-free for assembly or manufacturing for re-export, pull out. In just two years, 2008 and 2009, 300,000 jobs were lost.

Despite the recession that broke out in 2008 in the United States, economic growth has remained steady in El Paso, according to the U.S. Census Bureau.

Besides the immigration from Juárez, another factor fuelling the economy was the multi-billion dollar expansion of Fort Bliss, just outside El Paso, which is now the second largest military installation in the country and one of the main deployment centres for troops bound for Iraq and Afghanistan.

The River Divides Rich and Poor

The river between the two cities is increasingly a divide between rich and poor: those who can afford it flee to El Paso, and those who can't either stay in sprawling, ramshackle Juárez or return to their home cities and states.

"It's an exodus," said Rubio.

It was against that backdrop that Sergio Hernández was hit by a bullet to his head and bled to death next to a column under the Puente Negro bridge on the Mexican side of the practically dry riverbed, less than 20 metres from the border patrol officer who opened fire.

The officer's name has not been revealed.

Immigrants Face Increased Hostility

The increasingly hostile attitude towards immigrants is felt all along the border between the two countries.

On May 31, Anastasio Hernández, a Mexican construction worker, died three days after he was declared brain dead following a beating with a baton and tasering by U.S. border patrol agents at the San Ysidro border crossing between San Diego, California and Tijuana in Mexico.

Hernández, 42, was about to be deported to Mexico after nearly three decades living in San Diego. He and his wife of 21 years had five children born in the U.S.

Shacks in impoverished Juárez, Mexico, contrast sharply with the downtown financial district of nearby El Paso, Texas, seen in the background. © Danny Lehman / Corbis.

Another grainy amateur video, which captured his groans and shouts for help while he was being beaten, shocked Mexican society, which is demanding that the government of conservative President Felipe Calderón take a more vigorous stance towards Washington.

"There is a pattern of abuses of immigrants by U.S. authorities, which have surged in the years since September 2001, and are getting even worse now, since the Arizona law was passed," Rubio said.

The controversial SB (Senate Bill) 1070, signed into law on Apr. 23 [2010] in the state of Arizona, makes it a crime to be in the state illegally and allows state police to question and arrest people without a warrant if there is "reasonable suspicion" about their immigration status.

The number of Mexicans injured or killed by U.S. border patrol agents is on the rise, from five in 2008 to 12 in 2009 and 17 so far this year.

Young People Protest Sergio's Death

On Jun. 12, a group of around 30 youngsters from Juárez spray-painted graffiti on the Puente Negro bridge, sang songs and lit candles to protest Sergio Hernández's death.

"Some chavos (guys) jumped over to the U.S. side, there was a border patrol there and they yelled at them," said Alma, a young woman with the Zyrko Nómada de Kombate street artist collective, who took part in the demonstration.

"Then the feds (Mexican police) came, they stayed up there and said they were going to protect us, but told us not to throw stones," she told IPS.

The day of the demonstration, the bloodstain was still on the concrete where Sergio died.

Poverty Is on the Rise in US Suburbs

Alexandra Cawthorne

Alexandra Cawthorne is a research associate in the Poverty and Prosperity and the Women's Health & Rights programs at the Center for American Progress. She previously worked as a legislative assistant for the chairman of the US Senate Banking Committee, primarily on housing issues. She has also worked for the National Policy and Advocacy Council on Homelessness, the Poverty and Race Research Action Council, and the Citizens' Commission on Civil Rights.

In the following selection, Cawthorne states that the American suburbs are no longer the safe haven of economic security and prosperity that they once were. As a result of recent economic conditions, nearly one-third of the US poor now live in the suburbs. Midwestern cities and their suburbs have taken the brunt of this shift. Many of those who fled the cities for the suburbs in the 1990s are now facing recession-related challenges. Forty percent of foreclosures have displaced renters, who are both low-income and middle-class people. Cawthorne also notes that the suburbs do not have a safety net for the poor, and any services that do exist are stretched thin. Cawthorne's opinion is that innovative policies are needed to address growing suburban poverty.

The suburbs were once considered by many to be a retreat from poor economic and social conditions in cities. Now, however, they're home to nearly one-third of our nation's poor—and [that number is] rising. The last decade set in motion this shift in the map of poverty, but the recession exacerbated key economic trends that rapidly increased the growth rate of suburban poverty to more than double that of central cities.

Federal and state governments should take note: This emerging trend calls for a corresponding shift in poverty policies that includes a more regional, all-encompassing approach.

The numbers are startling. Analysis from the Brookings Institution found that since 2000 the number of poor people in the suburbs jumped by more than 37 percent to 13.7 million—also outpacing the national growth rate of 26.5 percent. In a reversal from the beginning of the decade 1.6 million more poor people lived in the suburbs of the nation's largest metro areas last year [2009] than in inner cities. Making matters worse, social service providers are often spread thin in suburban areas, and many have been forced to turn away more poor people as the need grows.

Some regions are having a harder time than others. Midwestern cities and their surrounding suburbs have seen the largest poverty rate increases since 2000. In the Chicago region, poverty rates are still higher in the city of Chicago than its surrounding suburbs. But the suburban counties are driving the growth of poverty in the Chicago six-county area. Chicago's surrounding suburbs experienced more than a 50 percent rate increase while the city's poverty rate actually declined by 0.9 percent. Research uncovered similar trends in more than half of the nation's largest metro areas.

Poverty Is Not as Apparent in the Suburbs

Poverty tends to be less visible in the suburbs and manifests differently from poverty in inner cities. Outer-ring suburban areas often have fewer community anchors such as universities, hospitals, and large businesses to stabilize them, which results in islands of poverty more isolated than the poor populations in many inner-city neighborhoods. Additionally, suburban communities have seen increased racial and income stratification as low-income workers—particularly recent immigrants and Hispanics—followed the migration of low-skilled and low-wage jobs out of central cities.

Concentrated poverty is still a significant problem even though it's not as pervasive as it once was. The number of high-poverty areas—the Census tracks those with poverty rates of at least 40 percent—declined by nearly 25 percent between 1990 and 2000. Certain actions helped: Changes in low-income housing policy, for example, including the expanded use of housing choice vouchers eased many poor families' mobility. At the same time, the gentrification of many city neighborhoods displaced low-income and working-class families that could no longer afford rapidly rising housing prices.

But over the last decade many low-income families leaving deteriorating high-poverty neighborhoods in central cities in search of better job opportunities, neighborhoods, and schools found themselves settled in new pockets of poverty in the suburbs. The decline in concentrated poverty varied across metropolitan areas as many poor households shifted from inner-city neighborhoods to outer-ring suburban areas. And poverty rates drastically increased in some suburban tracts as low-income families resettled outside of cities.

Suburban Downward Mobility

The downward mobility seen by a significant number of suburban residents since 2000 has gone largely ignored. A strong economy during the 1990s led to the development of super-sized subdivisions, "McMansions," and gleaming glass office towers beyond city limits in major metropolitan areas across the country. This may have led to the impression that all was well in the suburbs. But the social and economic challenges created by high poverty in cities increasingly spread to their surrounding counties during the 2000s. And as incomes have fallen in recent years the struggle to make ends meet has grown for everyone—especially among moderate- and middle-income households.

Suburban communities have been affected by a growing number of recession-related fiscal challenges including job loss, unemployment and underemployment, and the foreclosure crisis. But several issues intensify suburban poverty and create additional barriers to the economic well-being of people living in these communities.

Affordable Housing Is an Issue

Well before the current housing market instability low-income households faced numerous housing challenges including an absolute shortage of affordable housing units. The foreclosure crisis deepened these existing challenges, especially for low-income renters: Forty percent of foreclosures have displaced renters.

But the dearth of affordable housing is now a middle-class issue, too, particularly in the suburbs. One study from the University of North Carolina Center for Community Capital explains that the affordable housing crunch is no longer felt "primarily at the bottom of the income scale . . . it has moved with surprising rapidity and reaches well into the middle class."

Make no mistake: The very poor have the greatest housing need due to a severe lack of low-income and subsidized housing in most communities. But exclusively focusing on the lowest-income families ignores the millions of moderate-income families whose critical housing needs are sending their households into the ranks of the poor. And many of these families are increasingly relying on strained social safety net programs to make ends meet.

No Strong Safety Net in the Suburbs

Analysis from Brookings finds that poor people's requests to nonprofit groups for help making housing payments, paying bills, and purchasing food jumped 30 percent between 2008 and 2009 alone. Almost three out of four social service organizations reported requests from people who [had] never sought help before. These included suburban residents. What's more, the suburban safety net is often stretched thin across a larger service delivery area than its urban counterpart.

Most suburban nonprofits are also more fiscally constrained than ever before due to public and private spending cuts. Private charitable giving is also often not directed at poverty in the suburbs partly due to a perception that cities need more help.

Many outlying suburban areas don't have a public transportation system, and getting anywhere often requires a car. The lack of a personal vehicle and limited access to efficient public transportation is a significant barrier to employment for poor people in many suburban communities. Low-income families also need transportation to access supportive services, which are typically dispersed throughout a wide area.

The recession undoubtedly plays a big role in the suburbs' worsening poverty. Jobs are obviously priority number one. But tackling increasing poverty in the suburbs requires policy interventions that also address the lack of affordable housing, sparse supportive services, and deficient public transportation systems. Paying more attention to each of the above issues would help make life a little easier for suburban residents who've fallen on hard times.

Innovative Policies Are Needed

The remarkably high growth of suburban poverty contradicts our commonly held perceptions of suburbs as leafy subdivisions, gated communities, and, in general, refuges from poverty in cities. But this redrawing of the American poverty map should cause us to abandon long-held myopic views of the people and communities that typically see poverty's effects. Governments should work toward breaking down urban-suburban silos and develop innovative regional approaches to tackle poverty that encompass both city and suburb.

Haitians Live in Dire Poverty

Paul J. Sullivan

Paul J. Sullivan is a professor of economics at the National Defense University in Washington, DC. He also is an adjunct professor of security studies at Georgetown University.

Living like a disaster victim is nothing new to the average Haitian. The 2010 earthquake that devastated the island nation just brought more misery to the poorest country in the Western Hemisphere, states Sullivan in the following article. While corrupt officials and the very wealthy live well, most Haitians live on less than two dollars a day. Few sources of income, a lack of health care, and illiteracy are a part of daily life. Clean water and electricity are key to Haiti's survival, asserts Sullivan. Meanwhile, the need for wood fuel has led to deforestation and soil erosion that further complicate Haiti's resource issues. In order to turn around the intractable poverty of its citizens, Haiti needs leadership and ethical government.

The average Haitian has been living the life of a disaster victim even before the earthquake. It is the poorest country in the Western Hemisphere. Its human development and other indices were about what one would find in some of the poorest sub-Saharan [African] countries. Mismanagement, corruption and just plain venality have forever been human-caused security earthquakes in this sad country.

Jobs and Health Care Are Severely Lacking

The average GDP [gross domestic product] per capita in the country was about $600. However, if one calculates how much is owned by a very small percentage of the country, and how

Dr. Paul J. Sullivan, "Perspective: Water, Energy, Economy, Poverty and Haiti," Circle of Blue, January 28, 2010. www.circleofblue.org.

much of the GDP is made from these tightly controlled assets, then the GDP per capita for the average Haitian was much lower than $600. Maybe it was closer to $300–400. About 80 percent of Haitians lived on less than $2 a day while about 60 percent lived on less than $1 a day. Only about 50 percent of Haitians had some form of health care prior to the earthquake and about 3 percent had telephones. The very wealthy, the leaders of the street gangs, and the drug dealers lived very well amidst this grinding and spirit-crushing impoverishment.

Illiteracy Rampant, Job Skills Low

About 50 percent of Haitians were illiterate, and roughly 50 percent of the school-aged children were enrolled in school prior to the earthquake. Families needed their children to help keep the family from falling even further into the sinkhole that is poverty in Haiti. But, by lacking education, they remained stagnant, falling further. It is all so terribly sad.

Unemployment prior to the earthquake, and for many years previous to it, was about 50 to 60 percent. Skilled labor is scarce. The opportunities to get skills is even less. Most Haitians are trapped in the stagnant, debilitating addiction called chronic and intense poverty. The country has been on the economic life support of foreign and remittance labor from expatriates for years—now it is in economic cardiac arrest.

Six of the most important resource insecurities and paucities Haiti faces are energy, clean water, sanitation, deforestation, land degradation and coral reef degradation. These are all intimately interconnected in this land of devastation and destitution.

Very Few Have Access to Clean Water

About 70 to 80 percent of Haitians had no access to clean water prior to the earthquake. A very small percentage of people had access to piped water, and this was mostly in the cities. Sewer systems and wastewater treatment were close to nonexistent. Only the very rich or the very lucky had access to water treatment from privately-owned systems or from systems donated by well-meaning, but very much stressed NGOs [nongovernmental organizations] and aid organizations. There was little access to safe water and the rates of water poisoning from bacteria and disease were very high. Many children and others died from water-borne illnesses over the years. Maternal mortality was quite high in part due to the lack of clean water. In the rural areas only about 45 percent of the richest groups had access to safe water. Now think how the poorest live.

In all of this there is a stunning bit of data that also reminds me of Sub-Saharan Africa. Haiti uses only 8.3 percent of its available renewable freshwater resources (other sources peg this figure at 7.5 percent) even though many children in school and workers on the job often go the entire day with little to drink.

Lack of Electricity Stymies Progress

Only about 13 percent of Haitians had legal access to electricity. When you add in the stolen electricity maybe 25 percent had access to electricity. Electricity was produced by three small and decrepit thermal power plants, which are fueled by imported oil products since Haiti has no refinery, and a feeble hydropower plant in the hills near the Dominican Republic, the Peligre Dam, which took over 20 years to build and much less than that to rot into a shadow of its effective self.

Haiti had one of the lowest demands for electricity per capita in the world. It had the worst electrical system in the Western Hemisphere. The main port for importing the fuels for the thermal plants is damaged and the plants may also be quite damaged.

Electricity is needed for development. This has been proven time and time again. It is also needed to move water and to clean water. Safe water is hard to have without electricity or, at least, another reliable source of energy to clean and move the water. (To complete the sad circle of water and energy for Haiti: on a good year the Peligre Dam produces about one-third of the electricity produced in Haiti, but it has often been subject to the ravages of drought.)

Energy Infrastructure Needs Rebuilding

Given that Haiti is disaster prone maybe one of the best solutions for Haiti for its energy poverty and insecurity is to set up non-grid electricity. Some options include solar, wind, geothermal and other renewable and off-grid energy sources. Off-grid power is less prone to systematic collapse during and after disasters. It could also be a much less expensive way to improve electricity access to those in the rural areas and poorer areas of the towns and cities who have been outrageously underserved. Large electricity grid connections are very expensive to build and fairly easily subject to damage by natural and other disasters.

It is clear that Haiti's thermal and hydro generating stations are in grave need of repair and much better management and maintenance. It is also clear that for Haiti to rebuild it will need energy and lots of it. Right now it has very little financial, skill, management, administration and leadership capacity to make this happen.

Energy is required to clean and to move water. But, then again, you need the energy, finance and leadership to build the water transport and distribution system to get the clean water to the people first. In most areas of Haiti this does not exist. In many of the hill areas people relied on streams, often polluted and filthy, for their water. Piped water is rare in much of Haiti. And this is a country not far from our coast, and a neighbor in need.

Using Wood for Fuel Has Caused Deforestation

Energy starvation in Haiti has also been intimately related to deforestation, land degradation, coral reef ruination, and the lowering of fisheries and land agricultural yields. The main

An open sewer in Cite Soleil, a shantytown in Port au Prince, Haiti, a country where most people have no access to clean water, and where sewage systems and wastewater treatment are almost nonexistent. © Jenny Matthews / Alamy.

source of energy for Haitians has always been biomass. This has usually been in the form of charcoal briquettes and other energy forms developed from chopping down trees and gathering up agricultural and other waste for cooking, etc. The aching drive for energy has massively deforested the country. Attempts to turn this around seem to have had minimal impact relative to the overall problem.

As the trees were uprooted and destroyed, the best soils washed away. The ability of the land to hold the precious water of Haiti was also uprooted. Some of the soil that washed away went into the sea and damaged some of the coral reefs. This damaged some of the fisheries. There have also been devastating land- and mudslides. Expect more of these.

To be fair, however, if you were desperately poor and had no other way to cook, and you were illiterate and had no knowledge of the effects of your actions and you needed to do what was needed to do for your family's survival what would you do? Add to all of this that indoor cooking with biomass is a huge source of health problems in Haiti and we have a vicious circle of water, energy, land, and other resource poverty circling about in the midst of economic, educational and knowledge poverty, which is in turn circling about in health poverty.

Haiti Needs Assistance

Electricity, be it from grid power or from distributed solar, wind, etc. can also make medical clinics more viable. Energy helps keep medicines cool and helps sanitize the water, instruments, operating tables and more that are needed in hospitals and clinics.

The energy-water connections can help develop jobs and the dignity that goes with them. The negative synergy of interconnections amongst energy, water, land, food, health, jobs, education, leadership and more have led to devastation and destitution in Haiti so far. Those same synergies can be turned positive by the proper leadership, investments, training and education, for Haitians, and with considerable help from those outside of Haiti. In no way does the average Haitian have the financial capacity to rebuild after this.

Mismanagement, corruption and just plain venality are not victimless crimes. Poverty is not a victimless existence. Leadership is required to turn this situation around. Sadly, I doubt anybody expects this great and benevolent leadership to move into the crumbled presidential palace anytime soon.

The next time you leave the tap running and the lights on you might want to think of Haiti. Most people there can do neither and never could.

Western Culture and Materialism Lead to Depression

Robert J. Hedaya

Robert J. Hedaya is a medical doctor and clinical professor of psychology at Georgetown University Hospital in Washington, DC. Hedaya authored Understanding Biological Psychiatry *and* The Antidepressant Survival Program: How to Beat the Side Effects and Enhance the Benefits of Your Medication.

According to Hedaya in the following selection, Western culture, with its emphasis on material acquisition and competition for status, has eliminated humanity's connection to the rhythms of nature. As a result, people in Western cultures seek fulfillment in physical and material objects, performance, money, and status. Hedaya says people in Western society are more depressed than those in other cultures and have less attachment to a collective community as well as more health issues. In spite of their material possessions, they feel empty and directionless.

The physical world we have created and within which the incidence of depression is most rapidly rising is the densely populated Western city. It is made of concrete, steel, glass and asphalt. Most of us breathe hydrocarbon polluted air, eat nutritionally harmful or vacuous food (see your local fast food menu or supermarket tomato or strawberry for details), and drink plasticized bottled water. The National Institute of Health is studying over 900 new-to-nature chemicals, thought of as hormone interrupters, to see what effect they have on us.

Nature Is Absent from Daily Life

If we are fortunate, we may have an ocean retreat from the man-made. If we are less affluent we may make special trips to connect to nature, be it at the zoo, or the botanical gardens. But for most of us in most of Western civilization, nature is absent from our daily life. We and nature are strangers, distant relatives, and therefore we have become estranged from an important and deep aspect of our own natures. We do not, in a personal sense, understand nature as [American philosopher and author Henry David] Thoreau came to, when he was at Walden Pond. I experienced this for several years as an avid mountain biker. Year after year I would bike the same trails. I was foolishly surprised when, after a winter away, the forest had changed. Year after year, bit by bit, storm by storm. I began to notice the death and new growth, the re-working of the bike trails around nature's events.

Most of us do not know, in our bones, the slowly changing rhythms of the forest through the seasons, and year after year. We can only see time passing in the faces of our loved ones, or the mirror, but we do not experience the naturalness of the passage of time via a changing, slowly morphing landscape around us. We have lost the mirroring experience which the natural world provides us around the experience of time, the naturalness of it, as we might experience, if we lived connected to nature. And so we are left with an experiential void which is filled by a tremendous existential aloneness and anxiety about the strangeness of death, which seems quite disconnected from our lives, and therefore fails to inform our lives with meaning and value. We are no longer chaperoned through the stages of our lives by nature. And so we cling to youth, attempting to freeze time.

Materialism Fills the Void

In the purely physical universe, where there is no inherent meaning, and no dialogue with nature, we seek solace in the physical. We buy what we don't need, because it is supposed to make us feel good. We work harder to buy more, because it may make us feel better. Safer. In the process, we become alienated from our families (too much time at the office, too much pressure on performance which translates into money and purchasing power and ultimately, safety from financial anxiety), our coworkers (who are generally viewed as competition).

Furthermore, as a culture, Western society seems to have lost its center, and seems disoriented, and without a higher purpose. The capitalistic ethos seems to have replaced a constitutional, higher purpose or imperative.

And finally, we, as a society remain largely unconscious of the issues I have raised above, about our effect on other cultures, and on our planet. In the last 90 years, two world wars, multiple holocausts, threatened nuclear annihilation, and now a massive global imbalance are in the consciousness of each person on the planet. It is all very real, yet we, as individuals, as political parties, as families, communities and as a culture, are quite willing to be unconscious of the clear evidence that our current approach to human existence is failing. What is often said to alcoholics—the definition of insanity is doing the same thing over and over again and expecting a different result—can certainty be applied to Western civilization. Perhaps, with the current economic crisis, we have 'hit bottom'.

Rising Rates of Depression Are No Surprise

And so, to circle around to the point at hand—if one is living in a fundamentally imbalanced and insane culture, is it surprising that greater and greater numbers of individuals are presenting with depression? Should we be so myopically focused on the individual? Is that individual focus not part of the reductionsitic thinking that has limited the effectiveness of the current treatment approach? Can and should the individual carry the full burden for recovery from depression?

It seems that on a collective level, higher numbers of depressed non-functioning individuals are already causing a braking, or a negative feedback loop to the growth of the culture, via excessive health care costs, comorbid conditions such as diabetes and heart disease, and reduced viability of the individual, the family unit and therefore the community—all known sequelae [consequences] of depression.

If we can learn about and understand the links between the brain and the immune system, and between diet and mood, must we not wonder about the links between the culture and individual behavior, between the stresses of Western psychology and the craving for something to satisfy the inner emptiness? Is there not then a link between this craving, and the purchase of material goods (and the attendant stresses of paying for them), just as there is between the intake of sweets and the subsequent inflammatory response?

A Reconnection with Community Is Essential

Ultimately, reduction of the incidence and prevalence of depression on the public health scale will not come from antidepressants, individual psychotherapy, or from fish oil. It will come from a re-connection of the individual with the larger whole of the family, the community, a purposeful culture, and a dialogue with nature and meaning. This will require a rebalancing of the male-dominated, individualistic, domination oriented culture (in which reason and logic are the only way of knowing) with the feminine, wholistic, interactive and participatory approach to life. We, as human beings, need a balance of both to thrive. Socioeconomic and political efforts to incorporate such an integrated view of ourselves, the world and our futures are the therapy which this culture requires, if we are to stem the rising tide of depression.

In the many older cultures (e.g., Jewish, Indian), the collective community is responsible for the well-being and good behavior of the individual. So too, must the larger Western society and culture be held accountable for its role in the mental health and well-being of individuals.

For Further Discussion

1. In Chapter 1, Susan Shillinglaw discusses Steinbeck's views about ethnicity and how his attitudes are reflected in his writing. Do you think Steinbeck's portrayal of Mexicans and Mexican village life are stereotyped or romanticized? Explain your answer. Have you been the subject of stereotyping in your life? If so, how did you deal with it?

2. Sydney J. Krause in Chapter 2 argues that Kino exchanges enslavement to poverty for enslavement to material goods. Considering his overall economic status, do you think Kino made the right decision, or should he have considered alternatives? If so, what alternatives might you suggest?

3. In Chapter 2, Michael J. Meyer suggests that Kino and Juana are faced with a world of dualities, in which there are no easy answers. What dualities does he mention? Are there others you can identify? If you were faced with these choices, what would you decide and why?

4. Patricia Cohen and Paul Gorski in Chapter 3 offer different viewpoints about the culture of poverty. Do you think a culture of poverty exists? Why or why not? Cite from the essays in your answer.

5. Paul J. Sullivan in Chapter 3 describes the extreme poverty of most Haitians and solutions for improving their quality of life. Do you think wealthier nations have an obligation to help Haiti and other poor nations? Why or why not? If you had the means to help, what would you do first?

For Further Reading

Aravind Adiga, *The White Tiger: A Novel*. New York: Free Press, 2008.

Ernest Hemingway, *The Old Man and the Sea*. New York: Scribner, 1952.

John Steinbeck, *Cannery Row*. New York: Viking, 1945.

John Steinbeck, *The Grapes of Wrath*. New York: Viking, 1939.

John Steinbeck, *Of Mice and Men*. New York: Random House, 1937.

John Steinbeck, *Tortilla Flat*. New York: Book-of-the-Month Club, 1935.

John Steinbeck, *Travels with Charley in Search of America*. New York: Viking, 1962.

Bibliography

Books

Richard Astro   *John Steinbeck and Edward F. Ricketts:*
The Shaping of a Novelist.
Minneapolis: University of Minnesota
Press, 1973.

Richard Astro and *Steinbeck: The Man and His Work.*
Tetsumaro   Corvallis: Oregon State University
Hayashi, eds.   Press, 1971.

Jackson J. Benson   *The True Adventures of John*
Steinbeck, Writer. New York: Viking,
1984.

Jackson L.   *The Short Novels of John Steinbeck:*
Benson, ed.   *Critical Essays with a Checklist to*
Steinbeck Criticism. Durham, NC:
Duke University Press, 1990.

Thomas Fensch,   *Conversations with John Steinbeck.*
ed.   Jackson: University Press of
Mississippi, 1988.

Sunita Jain   *John Steinbeck's Concept of Man.* New
Delhi: New Statesman, 1979.

Cliff Lewis and   *Rediscovering Steinbeck: Revisionist*
Carroll Britch,   *Views of His Art, Politics and Intellect.*
eds.   Lewiston, NY: Edwin Mellen Press,
1989.

Scott J.   *Social Solutions to Poverty: America's*
Myers-Lipton   *Struggle to Build a Just Society.*
Boulder, CO: Paradigm, 2007.

Jay Parini   *John Steinbeck: A Biography.* New
                    York: Henry Holt, 1995.

Elaine Steinbeck   *Steinbeck: A Life in Letters.* New York:
and Robert   Viking, 1975.
Wallsten, eds.

John H.   *John Steinbeck's Fiction: The Aesthetics*
Timmerman   *of the Road Taken.* Norman:
                    University of Oklahoma Press, 1986.

Muhammad   *Creating a World Without Poverty:*
Yunus   *Social Business and the Future of*
                    Capitalism. Cambridge, MA:
                    PublicAffairs Books, 2008.

Periodicals and Internet Sources

Richard Astro   "From the Tidepool to the Stars:
                    Steinbeck's Sense of Place," *Steinbeck*
                    Quarterly, Winter 1977.

Roland Bartel   "Proportioning in Fiction: *The Pearl*
                    and *Silas Marner*," *English Journal,*
                    April 1967.

Roger Caswell   "A Musical Journey Through John
                    Steinbeck's *The Pearl*: Emotion,
                    Engagement, and Comprehension,"
                    Journal of Adolescent & Adult
                    Literacy, September 2005.

John Ditsky   "From Oxford to Salinas: Comparing
                    Faulkner and Steinbeck," *Steinbeck*
                    Quarterly, Fall 1969.

Natasha Gilbert   "Can Conservation Cut Poverty?,"
                    Nature, September 16, 2010.

Gerard J. Hasenauer	"Review of *La Perla*," *Modern Language Journal*, May 1950.
Carolyn Jaramillo de Montoya	"Poverty," *Journal of Pediatric Health Care*, November–December 2007.
Moushira Khattab	"Rethinking Poverty: Making Policies That Work for Children," *Children, Youth and Environments*, vol. 19, no. 2, 2009.
Peter Lisca and Lester Jay Marks	"Review of Thematic Design in the Novels of John Steinbeck," *American Literature*, January 1971.
Kerry Martin and Ruth Hart	"Trying to Get By: Children and Young People Talk About Poverty," *Poverty*, Summer 2011.
Charles R. Metzger	"Steinbeck's *The Pearl* as a Nonteleological Parable of Hope," *Research Studies*, June 1978.
Harry Morris	"*The Pearl*: Realism and Allegory," *English Journal*, October 1963.
Susan Shillinglaw	"Why Read John Steinbeck," The Steinbeck Institute, 2011. www.steinbeckinstitute.org/read.html.
Roy S. Simmonds	"Steinbeck's *The Pearl*: A Preliminary Textual Study," *Steinbeck Quarterly*, Winter–Spring 1989.
Chris D. Simms and D. David Persaud	"Global Health and Local Poverty: Rich Countries' Responses to Vulnerable Populations," *Canadian Journal of Public Health*, May–June 2009.

Francis C. St. John	*"La Perla,"* *Hispania*, August 1949.
Thomas Sugrue	"Steinbeck's Mexican Folk-Tale," *New York Herald Tribune*, December 7, 1947.
James W. Tuttle	"Steinbeck Remembered," *New Criterion*, March 1995.

Index